THE OREGON TRAIL IS STILL ALIVE

THE 1995 PHOTOGRAPHIC RETRACING OF THE 1853 TRAIL

KEN and LAURA JONES

Library of Congress Cataloging-in-Publication Data

Data Pending

SECOND EDITION

Published By:

Ken and Laura Jones
235 Terrace Street
Ashland, Oregon 97520

ISBN 0-9656614-0-7

STATEMENT OF CONFIDENTIALITY

iii

ACKNOWLEDGMENTS

The compilation of the diaries that make up this book would not be possible were it not for the historic material available to us, from historians, books, magazines, and brochures.

Specifically, we wish to acknowledge the following:

Western Oregon State College, sponsor of our Oregon Trail Tour

Oregon Historical Society, who published Nathaniel Myer's diary

Edward B Ham, who edited Nathaniel Myer's diary

Southern Oregon Historical Society for their research article of the Applegate Trail

Our fellow tour travellers, who made our Oregon Trail trip so special, providing us with photos, and video recordings, as well as stories and friendships that we will never forget!

PREFACE

During 1995, we retraced the steps of the early pioneers on the long Oregon Trail from the midwest to the Pacific Northwest. A group of history enthusiasts went with us.

The important milestones along the way were photographed and included herein. The path followed was based upon the 1853 diary of one of us(Laura Jones).

We have included a novel based upon the events that happened of the original pioneer trek.

The exciting events given here should be of extreme interest to the history buffs, historians, and the general public.

Laura and Ken Jones

Dec 24, 1996

CONTENTS

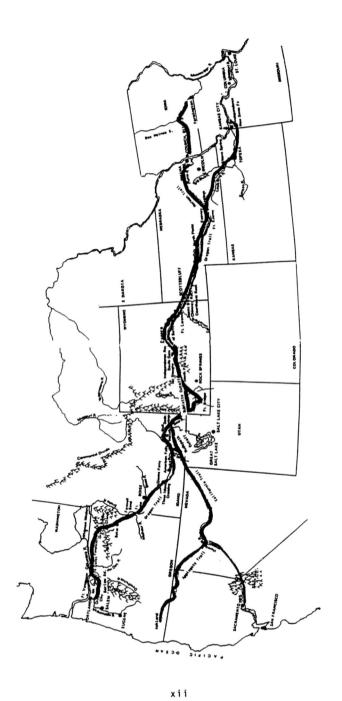

Figure 1   THE OREGON TRAIL

THE OREGON TRAIL IS STILL ALIVE

INTRODUCTION

The format of this book is rather unusual, for it is three stories combined
to tell the last one, the way it may have happened. The first is a diary of
Laura's great, great grandfather, which begins March 21, 1853, in Farmington,
Iowa. Farmington is located in the southeast corner of Iowa, close to the
Missouri and Illinois borders. This is the first day of the diary that takes
most of the Myer family, as well as others, on their five and one half months of
covered wagon adventure, ending in the Rogue River Valley of Oregon. Although
not mentioned, in his diary, it is interesting to note that the probable route
to begin with, was the Mormon Trail, which began a few miles east, probably at
Carthage, Illinois, passed close by Farmington on its way to Council Bluffs, and
off into the wilderness.

The second is a diary composed of tape recordings, and a journal made by
Laura and me, as well as a video tape provided by Stetson Hunt, a fellow R. V.
traveler on the tour, covering our three week caravan trek along the Oregon
Trail, which ended September 26, 1995 at Rickreall, Oregon, 142 years later.

The third is a story, reading between the lines of Nathaniel Myer's diary,
expanding on mentioned happenings, in an attempt to bring into focus the times
these people had, as well as thousands of other emigrants, traveling, one step
at a time, all the way to Oregon.

The date the Myer family left Farmington was important. The first day of
spring meant that the prairie grass would be growing for the animals to survive.
If the trip began too early, they would surely starve. Since the journey would
last five or six months, if they left too late, the snows of the Rockies, and

1

the Blue mountains of Oregon, could disastrously end in starvation and freezing. Many stories are told of this. While Nathaniel Myer authored the diary, his son, William Cortez Myer, was undoubtedly the instigator of the migration of the family to Oregon, as well as the wagonmaster. All, but one daughter of Nathaniel's, made the trip. Nathaniel was age 66, his wife, Mary, 61, Cortez, age 35, and his wife, Elizabeth, 33. The rest of the children, B. Franklin Myer, his wife, Dorothy (called Dolly), Temperance, widow of Thomas J. Gass, Elizabeth (later Mrs. E. K. Anderson), Sarah (later Mrs. A. G. Rockfellow), and Mary Ann, wife of Fruit Walker, wagonmaster of the accompanying Walker train, were between the ages of 17 and 36. In addition, nine grandchildren made the trip. The youngest, Frances(4 month old daughter of Cortez and Elizabeth, who later married G. F. Billings), was Laura's grandmother. Also included were seven hired men, along with five teams of four oxen each, two horse teams, and between seventy and eighty head of cattle.

Laura and I have been unable to ascertain the reason for the whole family to "pick up and move" to Oregon. Certainly, there appeared to be little reason for Nathaniel and Mary to make the trip. Since they lived in Ohio all of their married life, until they moved to Farmington in 1843, it may be that Nathaniel contemplated making the trip at that time. With all of the provisions, as well as a substantial sum of cash needed, it may well be that Nathaniel's assets made the whole thing possible. We are still trying to research this. We can conclude, however, that, if it were us, we would not want to be left behind, with all of our children and grandchildren going. Our primary reason for joining the R. V. caravan at Independence, Missouri, was to experience the Oregon Trail as closely as practical. We wanted to relate, in some way, to the life and experiences of Laura's ancestors, and the thousands of emigrants who came over two thousand miles, making indelible ruts in the trails to Oregon. We found the trail, or if gone, where it was, well marked with posts and monuments. Most of the time, we were on back roads, with many unpaved and dusty. Many reference books, diaries, and maps are available. We highly recommend the R. V. Caravan trip, sponsored by Western Oregon State College, but, with proper "homework", the trip can be made in most any fashion – just like the pioneers!

DIARY OF THE OREGON TRAIL TOUR

BY KEN AND LAURA JONES

AUGUST 31, 1995 – SEPTEMBER 26, 1995

AUGUST 31, 1995 – THURSDAY

After traveling from Ashland, Oregon to Independence, Mo., with our Ford pickup and Komfort fifth wheel trailer, we arrive at the beginning point of our Oregon Trail R. V. caravan tour back to Oregon. The adventure is sponsored by Western Oregon State college, and is limited to sixteen R. V.'s, including our "wagonmaster", and "tail gunner". Our "camp" for the next four days is located at the campus of the Reformed Latter Day Saints church. Our rigs are lined up side by side in a "parking lot" setting, but we do have full hookups. After securing our trailer, we enjoyed an organ recital at the RLDS temple. The temple appears to be new, with interesting architecture. The building is circular, with a tapering spire beginning at the third floor level, and ending several stories high. Inside, in the main auditorium, the ceiling is the spire, with windows spiraling to the top. The acoustics are superb, complementing the million dollar organ with 500 pipes. Because of this, the recital reverberated with sounds of resonance and discord. This evening we enjoyed a get-acquainted dinner at a local restaurant. Each of us were given the opportunity to introduce ourselves. We discovered we are a diverse group, representing most parts of our nation. There are three couples from Canby, Minnesota, and two couples from Illinois. The wagonmaster couple and the tail gunners had met once before this tour. The rest of us were not acquainted, but with this group, I feel we will become friends fast!

5

Fortunately, the rain, that had plagued us yesterday, has changed to sunshine, but it is quite humid. This is the day we have a bus tour covering the trail staging areas around Independence. The Santa Fe trail was used by the Oregon Trail followers, until it forks, with the Santa Fe going southwest and the Oregon Trail going northwest through, what is now, Lawrence, Kansas. our first stop is the Missouri river landing, where the emigrants disembarked from steamships carrying them, and their belongings up the river from St. Louis. Here they were able to purchase wagons, animals, and provisions, as well as form in "trains" for their journey west. There were a number of staging areas all the way to Council Bluffs, Iowa. The west side of the Missouri must have looked ominous to them, as the land was "Indian Territory", and undeveloped. Traveling along mostly back roads that follow the Santa Fe trail, our next stop is a monument stating "Santa Fe trail. 1821 –1872". Here we view depressions left from thousands of wagons, animals, and emigrants during their first day of travel. Now the area is grassy, and dotted with trees, some of which have grown in the swale. The next stop, on the Santa Fe trail, is the remains of Watts grist mill, located on Indian Creek. Here pioneers were able to buy flour needed for their long journey ahead. All that is left is part of the grist grinder, some foundation ruins, a monument, and, of course, Indian Creek. A shopping center encroaches the grounds. Our lunch break was at Gardner, Kansas, in the city park. Box lunches and soft drinks were provided. Our bus takes us further on the Santa Fe trail, until it forks with the Oregon Trail. Here, in rural Kansas, both trails still exist. We do see a number of oil wells dotting the landscape. With oil and fertile land, these farms are prosperous! We head on narrow gravel roads, the original Oregon Trail, to Lawrence, Kansas. At one point the trail makes a ninety degree turn for no apparent reason. In those

Figure 2 Assembling our Oregon Trail
tour group

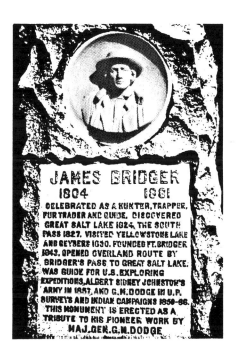

JAMES BRIDGER
1804   1881

CELEBRATED AS A HUNTER, TRAPPER,
FUR TRADER AND GUIDE. DISCOVERED
GREAT SALT LAKE 1824, THE SOUTH
PASS 1827. VISITED YELLOWSTONE LAKE
AND GEYSERS 1830. FOUNDED FT. BRIDGER
1843. OPENED OVERLAND ROUTE BY
BRIDGER'S PASS TO GREAT SALT LAKE.
WAS GUIDE FOR U.S. EXPLORING
EXPEDITIONS, ALBERT SIDNEY JOHNSTON'S
ARMY IN 1857, AND G.M. DODGE IN U.P.
SURVEYS AND INDIAN CAMPAIGNS 1859-66.
THIS MONUMENT IS ERECTED AS A
TRIBUTE TO HIS PIONEER WORK BY
MAJ. GEN. G.M. DODGE

Figure 3 Jim Bridger grave site
Independence, MO.

Figure 4   Watts mill at Indian Crk.

Figure 5   Parting of Santa Fe and
Oregon trails

days, there were no farms; just prairie and trees. I speculated that there could have been a large Indian encampment, requiring the turn! By the time we reached Lawrence, we had travelled a little over fifty miles. The pioneers had been on the trail for five or six days! I wondered why the emigrants felt that Oregon had more to offer than this rich Kansas farm land. It must have been the "carrot" offered by the U.S. Government, of free land to U.S. citizens coming to Oregon. Our country wanted to develop the Oregon territory with U.S. settlers, for, at that time, it was jointly claimed by the U.S. and England. Were it not for the settlers, it may have become under British control. We quickly returned, via I-70, to Westport, the original part of Kansas City, Missouri. Here, we enjoyed a brew at Kelly's bar,located in the oldest building in Kansas City. Our last stop was at Jim Bridger's grave site. He was one of the great mountain men of the west, and played an important role as a guide, and trader for the wagon trains.

SEPTEMBER 2, 1995 – SATURDAY

After breakfast in our R. V.'s, the group walked a few blocks to the National Frontier Trails Center. First, we enjoyed an interesting movie giving the history of the Santa Fe and Oregon trails, followed by a tour of the museum. The many artifacts and exhibits, concerning the great migration along the trails, help us to realize the overwhelming task these pioneers faced. This afternoon we visited the exhibit of the sunken steamboat,"Arabia", which sank when hit by a snag in the Missouri River in 1856. It may very well have been carrying passengers headed for the Oregon Trail! A family, along with some friends, became interested, and began uncovering it in 1989. Since its demise over 130 years earlier, the river has changed its channel, leaving the ship forty five feet below a corn field! In addition to the passengers, the ship carried a cargo, which included merchandise that a general store at that time, would stock. Amazingly, most of the goods were still intact, and thousands of items are displayed. We would certainly recommend this exhibit as one of the attractions of the Kansas City area. We were back at our campsite by 5:00pm.

SEPTEMBER 3, 1995 – SUNDAY

Sunday is a free day to relax and get our R. V.'s ready for departure the next day. Our friend, and Laura's former high school teacher, Mary Gean Forgus, and her daughter, Ann, live in the Kansas City area. They picked us up at 10:00 a.m., at our camp site, for a tour of Kansas City, which included an excellent brunch at a restaurant called "First Watch". After brunch, they showed us many of the points of interest. We particularly enjoyed some of the statues and sculptures for which the city is famous. After visiting both of their homes in Raytown, a Kansas City suburb, we were back by 3:00pm, in time to prepare for tomorrow's journey. The weather is still hot and humid.

SEPTEMBER 4, 1995 – MONDAY

Today is an exciting day. After a briefing at 7:30am, we formed a caravan, with our R. V.'s, for the beginning day of the Oregon Trail! I envisioned Laura's ancestors, the Myers getting their wagons and animals in caravan for their first day on the trail. I am sure that their emotions were filled with excitement, but also a great deal of trepidation. We could feel a degree of this for what was ahead of us! Most of us have not traveled in R. V. caravans, and some of us have had no experience with C.B.'s. Our wagonmasters, Russ and Rita, from Corvallis, Oregon, had us get in line by alphabetical order behind their Safari Trek 24' motor home. After the first day the line would move forward, with the front R. V. going to the rear. The wagonmaster and tail gunner maintained their positions of front and back, respectively. Since we would be traveling on dusty roads much of the time, changing positions would help "even up" the amount of dust each of us would endure. I had to wonder if the wagon trains did this. Since they were an independent bunch, I had my doubts! We all have C.B. names, with the first day lineup as follows: the wagonmasters, "Meadow Muffin", followed by "Bonnie and Clyde",(Dick and Bonnie), from Long Beach California, in their 30' Winnebago motor home, "Bob and Arlene",(Bob and Arlene) from Canby, Minnesota, with their 31' Airstream trailer, "Joe and Reta",(Joe and Reta) from Laguna Hills, California, in their 27' Sea Breeze motor home, "CJ"(Chuck and Virgene), from West Hills, California, towing a 31' Airstream, "Weare Bear and Coffee Lady"(Stet and Edythe), from Weare, New Hampshire, in their 34' Winnebago motor home, and towing a pick-up, "Komfort"(Ken and Laura), from Ashland, Oregon, pulling our 24' Komfort fifth wheel, "One Eyed Jack"(John and Patty), from Salina, Kansas, in their 35' Holiday Rambler, and towing a pick-up. "Big Lou"(Bob and Louise), from Yakima, Washington, in their 32' South Wind, and towing a Jeep Wagoneer, "Baby Chick"(Benny and Irene), from Canby, Minnesota, pulling a 31' Holiday Rambler trailer, "H2 E2"(Herb and Eleanor), from Canby, Minnesota, pulling a 28' Jayco fifth wheel, "Motormouth"(Ralph and Janet), from Half Moon Bay, California, towing a 25' Vacationer fifth wheel, "Double E and Walking Lady"(Ev and Juanita), from New Windsor, Illinois, pulling their 23' Airstream trailer, "Mayflower"(John and Josephine), from Leaburg, Oregon, in their 21' Le Sharo mini motorhome, "Bulldozer and Basket Lady"(Don and Liz), from Peoria, Illinois, towing their 30' Avion, and bringing up the rear,"Tail Gunner"(Vic and Nancy), from Sequim, Washington, towing a 30' Elite fifth wheel. Just imagine sixteen rigs, all in single file, heading down the road! Amazingly, we all made it through the busy Kansas City traffic, and entered the freeway to Lawrence. The weather is hot and sticky, aggravating our anxieties of staying together, and not"screwing up"! All went well to Lawrence, where we stopped for a twenty-minute coffee break. Shortly after passing through Topeka, on Highway #40, "CJ" suffered a flat tire on the trailer. The caravan pulled to the side of the highway, while some of the group assisted Chuck in replacing his tire. Within thirty minutes we were back on the highway. Now, we are traveling on a dusty road, following the Oregon Trail through rich farm land. Our next stop is Vieux Cemetery. The Vieux family operated a toll bridge, used by the emigrants to cross the Red Vermillion River. It is said that the Vieux family became wealthy from the toll fees. At this stop, we fixed lunch in our own R. V.'s. The highlight of the day was our stop at Alcove Spring. This was a "watering hole" used by the pioneers, and made famous by the Donner party. They were delayed here a week, waiting for better river crossing conditions for the Big Blue River. While they were there, they buried one of their kin. A stone monument tells the sad story. We ended our first day of R. V. travel at Marysville, Kansas. It took the wagon trains two weeks to reach this point! Our camp was the city park, with no hook-ups. After a chicken dinner in town, we attempted to rest through the hot humid night, with no air conditioning. Freight trains, loaded with coal, ran every few minutes, all night long. Our discomfort was trivial compared to that of the weary emigrants, camped here on the prairie.

Figure 6   Kansas Historical Marker

Figure 7   Marysville, KS City Park
Our RV's

13

NATHANIEL MYER DIARY

The following diary entries are taken from Nathaniel Myer's original journal,
and edited only to the extent needed to add what was the obvious intent of the
entry.

Farmington Township, Van Buren, Iowa

March 21st 1853. I left my dwelling bound for Origon Stoped at my son B Franklin
the first night

March 22; Clear morning the men are all ingaged in fixing and loading the wagons
Stayed all night

23; The following persons left Franklin viz my son Cortez his wife and daughter
Franklin his wife and two sons and one daughter Temperance and her son and four
daughters mother two daughters and self seven young men togather with 5 ox teams
each team 4 yoke two horse teams and between 70 & 80 head of neat catle Encamped
at Fordyce,s

24th Had a good nights rest All things went all well Our tent well we fixed one
of our stoves in it which keeps it warm with little fuel This afternoon I helped
to dirve the cattle Camped near the Indiana Hotel in Jefferson county 15 miles
from the former encampment Rested well

25 Cloudy morning The wind from the N.E. Cortez got Walker dog and lost him
again yesterday Clear in the afternoon High wind from the west. Elizabeth helped
to drive the catle in the forenoon Sarah drove the two black mares all day. The
roads considerably better than I expected them Encamped near Agency City, I rode
all day in a wagon Felt considerably unwell

26th Last night & this morning the wind blowed hard from the west This morning
cloudy I am considerably refreshed slept well Disagreeable day. Snowed rained
and blowed The roads bad, the team stalled several times The sun shone in the

evening encamped before sunset I drove the two blaks all day Made 13 miles

27th Clear morning the ground froze. The road tryer and more rolling then yesterday Encamped 3 miles E. of Oscolusa in Mahaska County Made 13 miles I drove the two blacks They are getting gentle

28th Clear and frosty morning Cortez has bought 4 cows and four or 5 hiefers since we left home He as soon buy on Sunday as any other day This day bought two black mares and one calf. Last night one of our oxen took sick We left him to die The road is some places dusty A few bad mud holes Encamped 9 miles west of Oskaloosa Sarah and myself drove the two black mares South wind at sunset & cloudy

29th Cloudy Wind S.E. Last night one of the helfers drop a dead calf. All well except Jackson. He is some better in the evening. Clear in the afternoon Encamped 6 miles west of Pella on the public road One of the oxen lame & another one purged considerable

30th Cloudy. Jackson,s complaint appears to be the mumbs Elizabeth helped in the forenoon to drive the cattle and Temperance in the afternoon Jackson rode in fore part of day in a wagon Drove his team in the afternoon. Smith was kiked by one of the black mares Made 16 miles Encamped 11 miles west of Fools Point Jasper County

31st Clear Jackson not fit for duty Smith on duty with some difficulty One of the hiefers run off last night Franklin gone after it Had to gard our stock last night Franklin found the hiefer Near 12 o clock came to Walkers were encamped. Encamped about 1/2 mile from Walkers camp Walkers all well Saw George Sturdevant Gave him his letter and bundle that his father send by me. Made 5 miles

April 1st Cloudy Cleared off about 10 o clock a.m. Stayed in our camp this day Women & men washed their clothes

S.2nd Clear morning All well Rained in the afternoon & in the night Remained at camp

S.3rd Cloudy at s.r. Jackson still not fit for duty. Remained in camp

M.4th White frost & clear I remained in camp Jackson on duty in afternoon

T.5th Clear morning High wind from the west blowing a constant gale Some of Walkers boys and our went about 4 miles to build a fence for a yard for all the stok The wind blowing so hard that they could not get it to stand. They had to abandon it and came back to their several encampments about 4 o clk p.m. This day received a letter from Enoch He was within 50 miles of Bluffs The news not flattering for our business

W.6th Clear at s.r. High wind last night Stayed at the camp all day Enoch came to camp last night From his report we concluded to remain on this side of river 7 or 8 days more Fodder & corn cheaper then on the other side

DIARY OF THE OREGON TRAIL TOUR

KEN AND LAURA JONES(continued)

SEPTEMBER 5, 1995 – TUESDAY

Marysville is an interesting, historic, community of about 3,400 residents. With an elevation of 1154 feet, it is located in the northeast agricultural area of Kansas, at the junction of highways #36 and #77, about 15 miles south of the Nebraska border. Among other distinctions, Marysville claims the first state post office(November 11, 1854), and was the home of the first state bank in Kansas. The town is also known for its black squirrel population. We enjoyed them at the city park, where we camped. A Marysville brochure states that the city has an ordinance protecting them, and one is included in the official city flag. Our first stop of the day is a visit to the Pony Express Park, just west of Marysville. The Pony Express took over where the railroad ended at St. Joseph, Missouri. Stations were located every few miles along the two thousand mile route, mostly on the Oregon Trail, to Sacramento, California. The Pony Express started in 1860, and, though not very profitable, filled the mail needs of the west until the railroad and telegraph stretched west to replace them. Marysville has the only home station left at its original site. Our second day on the trail, we are beginning to gain a little confidence in maneuvering our rigs in tight places, such as the parking area at this Pony Express Park. We managed to park all sixteen R. V.'s around the driveways and parking area. It is an impressive sight, and we are starting to feel the camaraderie of our new friends. Hollenburg ranch, our next stop, is a real treat. This is another station of the Pony Express, and claims to be the only unmoved, unrestored station still in existence. It gave us the feeling of living here one hundred and thirty years ago. The station is manned by volunteers of the Kansas unit of

17

the Pony Express Riders Association, an organization dedicated to preserving its history. For our benefit, two riders, with their trained horses, put on a demonstration of the changing of horses and riders. The weather is still very hot and humid, which, I am sure, made the horses and riders uncomfortably warm. We all appreciated their efforts. Horses were exchanged about every fifteen miles, and riders every seventy five miles or so. Mail was delivered from St. Joseph to Sacramento in about ten days, at a cost of $5.00 for 1/2 ounce. Riders were paid $25.00 a week. After the demonstration, we were treated to a pastry called calachies(similar to a butterhorn), along with coffee and tea. These were made and served by the volunteer women. It gave us all a chance to visit with these special hosts, leaving us with a much greater awareness of this part of our western history. Our lunch stop, Rock Creek Station, Nebraska, was a popular pioneer resting place. The station was made famous by "Wild Bill" Hickock, who killed several people here, over a money matter. The area, now a state park, has well defined trail ruts leading down to the buildings by the creek, that housed the Pony Express and freight stations.(ca 1861) A recently built visitor center is also here. Our last visit of the day was outside of Fairbury, Nebraska, at the grave of George Winslow, who died, on the trail, from cholera, in 1849. Our campsite, Crystal Springs Park, at Fairbury, has water and electricity, allowing us to escape the heat with air conditioning. Too far to walk, we climbed into several vehicles for the ride to the Courtyard restaurant for a delicious ham and roast beef dinner. I guess we can worry about the pounds and cholesterol after this trip! Fairbury has a population of about 4,300. Situated at an altitude of 1,315 feet, it is located at the junction of highways #15 and #136, a little north of the Kansas border. We have traveled, on back roads, seventy–one miles since leaving Marysville. While not noticeable, we are gradually climbing as we journey west. Now we are about three hundred feet higher than our departure point of Independence, Missouri, a distance of two hundred thirty eight miles(via back roads). Fairbury has some colorful murals painted on the walls of some business buildings. They depict the town during its early days. One shows the business district, with a parade of circus animals, and spectators lining the street; a familiar scene when the circus comes to town! After viewing these, we enjoyed watching the Chimney Swifts circling the chimney of one of the downtown buildings. One by one, they would dive into the chimney for their night's lodging. Laura and I had never experienced this before. We can feel the enthusiasm build in all of us, as we settle into our Oregon Trail adventure! SEPTEMBER 6, 1995 - WEDNESDAY

We awoke at 5:00 a.m. to thunder and lightning, with rain beginning to fall. The windows were open in the pickup, causing me to dash out in my pj's to close them. By the time we were up at 6:00 am the rain had stopped, bringing on a warm, muggy day. A breeze kept us comfortable. We moved out of camp at 9:00 a.m., traveling dirt roads along the Oregon Trail. Our first stop was an old school house, where we were greeted by a local couple, who gave us the history of the school, and the area. The Oregon Trail passes by here, as well as the Pony Express. A mile or so down the road, we stopped to view some traces left of the trail. I took a picture, which included the school in the distance. We followed the trail along dusty roads to our lunch stop at a little ghost town called Oak; population seventy-six. We continued on back roads, through rolling hills of farm country to Fort Kearny. The fort was built to provide protection, shelter, and provisions for the pioneers, as they headed west. It was here that the Myer wagon train connected with our route. They arrived here on May 21, 1853, two months after leaving Farmington, Iowa. This compares to our three days! A very pretty Fort Kearny State Park was our camp for the night. We are tired, and ready to rest. Laura's thoughts imagined what her ancestors felt, when camped here one hundred forty-two years ago!

Figure 8   Pony Express -Hollenberg
            Station - near Marysville,
            KS

Figure 9   The School on the Oregon Trail

Th.7th Clear at s.r. Froze ice this day Went to a new encampment about 5 mil in company with Walkers to find out a field of corn Beautiful day The boys all in their shirt sleeves This and the next page was omitted in its regular order On the 11th we had the first rain of any account Our tents turned the rain well So did the wagon covers I discovered some defects in all our wagon beds which could be easaly remeded in building them simply by extending the sides flush with the botom At present the sides rest on the botom boards This causes the water droping from the covers on the sides and entering into the wagon botoms and wetting any articles laying in the botom

F.8th Cloudy at s.r. Our encampment is a Everets in Polk county High wind Cortez & Fruit each took a wagon Went 3 or 4 miles to get oats in the sheaf Clear from 10 o,clk to 3 Sat

S.9th Clear at s.r. Froze ice 1/4 in thick last night Remained in camp

S. 10. Clear at s.r. Froze ice 1/4 in thick Hazy in the afternoon The men took all the cattle to a new stalk field about a mile from camp I got some papers to read from a neighbor Latest date March 22d. Jiles wells came to our camp about 4 o,clk p.m. His encampment is 8 miles east

M.11th Cloudy at s.r. A few drops of rain fell last night and this morning from 10 o,clk a.m. It rained moderately until night and during the night Wells encamped about one mile south of us He lost one of his fine hiefers this morning by death

T.12th Cloudy Thunder last night and yesterday Cloudy all day with some rain The cattle pen in bad condition on account of the rain that fell yesterday and last night

W.13th Clear at s.r. Wind west Thunder and rain last night The cattle broke out

22

of their pen last night All hands gathered to bring them back again Their pen still in a worse condition The cattle were all turned into the stock field in the evening About 10 o,clk a.m. It became cloudy and blustery Snowed some

Th 14th Clear Froze ice 1/2 in thick I went with Fruit to Wells camp They were all in good spirits Fruit and Enoch are gone to make ingagement with the ferrymen to ferry the wagons and stock across the Des Moines River Cortez & some of his men branded the horses and catle Fine day Smith one of our men has been sick for some days He went to a neighbor house Mother went to see him in the afternoon

F 15th Cloudy at s.r. Continued cloudy all day High winds from the east Lyzander Stone came to Walker camp His train including his fathers intends to encamp about 3 miles west of us This evening our invalids are getting better Smith returned to camp

S.16th Cloudy at s.r. Rained moderately the larger part of last night Silas Stone came to our camp Continued cloudy and cool all day

S.17th Clear at s.r. White frost Vegidation backwards and slow if any We pitched our tents on the bank of the Des Moine River on the farm of stoneburners about 2 miles from our last encampment Still in company with Walkers All the wagons and tents of both companies are close together Beautiful afternoon Lysander Stone came to our camp at noon Eat dinner and went on his business Smith on duty Fidelity & Mary stone came to our camp in the evening and two of their cozens named Hall

M.18th. Cloudy at s.r. The horse wagons and the loose horses of both trains crossed the Des Moines River and encamped near Carlisle about four miles from the last place About 12 m. It began to thunder and rain A new and bad road

Tu.19th Cloudy at s.r. Rained & thunder last night The few that were here had a tolarable nights rest The tent and wagoncovers turned the rain well Our camp is

23

on the farm of Mr Burget In Warren County The remainder of our & Walker train came on Wells train Is here also 31 wagons left and passed 150 head of loose cattle by our encampment this day The sun shone part of the day

W. 20th. Clear at s.r. Walkers & my boy bought a Durham bull 10 years old at $67 yesterday The sire of all the fine stock In this neighborhood Wells started before we did The horse teams and cattle next Came 13 miles encamped Mrs Walker,s and Martha horses got scared Run a short distance before they could stop them No Injury done One of our horses In the spring wagon got swamped in one of the many sloughs we crossed By the help of the other drivers we extricated him without andy great difficulties One of the black mares lost the right fore shoe In one of the mudy places Cloudy and some rain about 3 o,ck p.m. The cattle all on hand The ox also broke one yoke Double teamed In some bad places Silas stone & lady lodged in their wagon In our camp Lysander incampment 1/2 mile east

Th 21st Cloudy at s.r. Between 2 o,ck & s.r. a.m. heavy thunder storm & rain Made 10 miles Rained nearly all day The road some better then yesterday Our encampment on favorable ground Madison County

F. 22nd Cloudy High wind all last night 4 1/2 mile west of Winterset At Winterset saw two of wells girls 6 miles west of Winterset Clear afternoon Enoch with two and one of our wagons went to get corn to meet the train the morrow night One of our men(Stephan Thrash) has been sick for 4 or 5 days We have to hawl him on a wagon He had been considerable better This morning he ate some which did not agre with him he has been quiet sick since then Franklin and one of the boys stoped at Winterset to get some repairs done to the old wagon

S.23,d Last night It thundered rained and blowed Continued all this day Last night Walkers and us put up five tents this morning they were all blowed down but two The women and men made shift to get some breakfast such as it was Mother

Lizy and all the children and myself remained in the wagons The bed clothes in the wagon are considerably damp and wet The mens beding all wet About 8 o,clk a.m. we for a new encampment as we had no fead for our stock Arrived at the crossing of Midle River Not portable The men all engaged to fix the encampment Its raining and blowing Enoch & the men with him are here with the corn for the stock The men are in good spirits apparently The women children and myself are yet all in their wagons at 4 o,clk p.m.

S. 24th Rained nearly all night Snowed in the morning Three of Walkers men sick The men are engaged in cutting down Linn trees for the stock No corn to be had here this morning at any price Three of our calves died last night & one about dying The sun shone in the afternoon Two of Walkers oxen strayed off Enoch is gone after them The cattle were swum accross the river The horses wagons and tents remained on the same side

M. 25th Clear at s.r. White frost The women all engaged airing the bed and other cloth which they much need The rain and storm wetted a good many of them the two previous nights and one day There came 22 wagons this day near our encampment The men belonging to them commenced building two bridges across the river One to take the loaded wagons across The other a foot bridge 20 wagons crossed the river on the briges they constructed Adair County. Few inhabitants in the county

T 26th Clear at s.r. Still continues cool Vegidation slow no corn for catle Some for the Horsses About 10 1/2 o,clk we got all our wagon over the bridge built yesterday by the men mentioned They charged 25 cents per wagon for the use of it our men doing all the labor The bridge consist simbly by two logs agross the stream so far apart that wheels are outside of the logs The wagons are then placed on the logs with their load by hand then drawn by oxen across sliding on their axels on the logs Their were between 20 & 30 wagon on the other side at the time we got across Two wagon loads of corn came for us. Heard Enoch. He has not found his oxen yet He is still in search of them. We that is Cortez and Franklin has lost at this place in all five yearling calves After we crossed the bridge and paid the toll others came and posession of it and crossed over it without paying toll There was a good teal of jangling about it There were about 40 wagon taken acros after we crossed The Jiles Wells train came in the evening Oposite the river the men packed the corn over the river on their baks Wells got his wagons on this side of river Enoch got his oxen this evening

 W 27th Cloudy at s.r. Thunder and rain last night Part of the day clear Went about 3 miles Encamped on the border of timber The loose stock both catle and horses had been drove here yesterday in order to get some grass All hand are out that can be spared from the tents hunting the stock in order to get them closer togather Part of this day was clear and warm wind south and cloudy near sunset Two of our men on the sick list The best two we have in company Wells are ahead of us

Th.28th Cloudy at sunrise Thunder & rain last night moderately Made 18 miles and encamp at Notoway Creek Crossed two bad sloughs At one of them Fruits 4 horses got swamped The rest of the teames got through All the wagon beds took in some water At the other Enoch and our spring wagons brok some the the toung riggins Being in the prairie, with the aid of lines we fixed them up in such a manner that we came to this encampment

F 29th. Clear a s.rise and all day Our encampment being near the timber we fixed in the new our tong riggins with some addition of wooden pices and hickory poles well twisted Answered the purpose well Encamped in the prairie near a slough. Grass scarce, corn for the work oxen & horses which we hawl with us Made 10 mi

S.30th. Clear & windy at sunrise Cool Since our tong riggins brok we used only two horses Three of our men being sick Sarah drove the two teams in the spring wagon The day before yesterday Stone,s bull gave out Yesterday Franklin went back and found him Made such arrangement that Stone will get him. Yesterday Fruit started toward the Bluffs. Last night some of Walkers loose horses strayed off. J. Walker and Cortez went in search of them This day and the two previous days I saw a number of elk horns Some of the large growths Encamped in prairie Made about 10 miles Met two bad places The rest of the road was fine Near our encampment is a section post marked s.16:17 t75n.r36.w 20:21 J. Walker and Cortez came to the camp near sunset with horses that strayed away the last night. Grass poor

S May 1st Wind blowed hard last night and this morning. Tent blowed down in the night Tremendious rain storm at 7 o,clock am. Forded Nationobodomy Brok two standard on the little wagon Mr Walker lost some of his plates in crossing, Encamped in the botom of a branch of the same stream. Grass still scarce. No corn for the catle Half allowance of corn for horses Made about 8 miles

M 2nd. Clear at sunrise, all day Crossed on a very dangerous bridge with all the teams catle and horses without any injury Made 8 miles Encampment in prairie, Cass County Grass scarses, water plenty The work oxen & catle are doing tolarable well Fruit returned from the Bluffs

T.3rd Clear all day SE wind. Made 8 miles good road. Crossed one stream on a bridge, these bridges are made by the emigrants Bought 8 bus. corn at $1.50 per bus. Camped on or near a stream 15 Indians came to our camp, beging money & bread We gave them not anything The soil & face of the country is different here then in Van Buren and the water streams in perticular Soil sand Country rolling Streams narrow & deep with high bank and mine bank Streams 10 feet wide have to be bridged Road dusty Saw plum trees in bloom

W.4th Cloudy at sunrise Rained moderatly Two more Indians came to camp before we started Made 15 miles Encamped at Silver Creek about 4 o,clock pm. All hands engaged to build a bridge across the creek to cross over all the catle and

horses to paster for the night. On this days journey we crosedt one toll
bridge which was good and crossed two other bridges which were bad Lamed at one
of them one of the black mares At our encampment are plenty of wood and water
Got the horses & catle all over the bridge we mde.

Th 5th Cloudy at sunrise Clear in the afternoon Seen ten Indians going the same
way we did. Encamped in the Misourie botom near Kansville Made 18 miles. Some
bad road. Brock one wagonwheel No grass of any account

F.6 Cloudy, clear alternately Crossed the Missourie River with all the train
without any accident Went about three miles crossed a slough Some of the wagons
took in some water Found a good camping Wood & water convenient Grass scarse
Walker brock one of their ox wagon tong

S.7th. Clear & cool Vegidation is retarted these days Our sick men all on duty
except Thrash Seen several poor Indians at a slough demanding toll for a tempory
bridge they made We paid them 50 cents for the whole train Made 4 miles to
tolaraable good grass All hand engaged in airing the cloths and fixing the loads
in the different wagons with the additional articals bought at Canesville. One
of Mrs Walkers oxen was missing this morning Enoch went in search of him Found
him Returned near sunset

S.8th Clear and cool Not favorable for grass which we so much need Cloudy and
some rain High wind from the west. Made 12 miles. Encamped near a slough. Plenty
of water Wod scarce, grass midling. George Sturdivant sick

M.9th Cold winday day. Crossed several emigrants bridges Feried Elkhorn River
Paid $5 per wagon and $1 per horse. We swam the catle and horses without any
injury but not without much labor Made 12 miles Encamped in a bad place in the
botom of the river Grass tolarable good. The road dusty part of the way

T.10th White frost Two Indians at the camp at breakfast, beging salt bread &
meat We gave them some of each In the forenoon the road soft & wet in the

afternoon the road was equal to a plank road Made 18 miles Camped in the prairie
Had water No wood to cook Super with try course grass. Grass midling Rained in
the night

W.11th Clear High wind from the north Made 15 miles Had good roads Only two
sloughs not difficult. We headed one bad and difficulte. Encamped in prairie.
Wood, water & grass good

Th 12th. Clear cool morning Warm in the afternoon Crossed Shell Creek bridge
Crossed several bad sloughs The road beautiful sandy and dusty. The western part
of Iowa sandy and the sand increasing as we have advanced westward Made 16
miles encamped in prairie Found some wood Bad water The grass not as good as we
had last night at Shells Creek bridge Saw 8 or 10 Indians asking toll We gave
them not anything. We saw at once that the bridge was built by the emigrants

F 13th. Clear at sunrise Changed to thunder and a few drops rain at m Passed
some of the beautiful prairie Good road, a fewsloughs not bad Made 16 miles
Encamped in the bottom of the Loup Fork Plenty of wood water Grass across a
slough Had to make a bridge to pass the stock over

S.14th Thunder & rain last night. Cloudy at sunrise. We now travel up the Loup
Fork The ferry is below. We concluded to ford it at some distance up it. Not
much out of our rout A tremendious storm of wind and rain. The wind continued
untill night. Blowed Enochs sleeping wagon cover into several pieces. Mrs
Walkers carrige top was taken down to keep it from upsetting She & her daughter
had to take the storm in her open carrige. Crossed Beaver Creek Good ford, water
rather deep. Some of the wagons beds took some water. Made 12 miles Encamped
near the River Loup Wood and water some 1/4 mile from camp Grass poor

S.15th Clear morning Crossed a stream 16 feet wide on a bridge Also Cedar Creek
100 feet wide 2 1/2 feet deep We forded it Good ford Ee can see the Walker
trains that crossed at the ferry from where we are encamped inside of Loup Fork

near a beautiful lake No wood only what we brought with us Made 14 miles Passed
a number of ravines country more rolling

M.16 Clear at sunrise. Thunder and rain last night. Thunder & rain between one
and two o,clock pm Forded Loup Fork The water not to deep The route across is
1/2 mile from where you go in and come out. Jackson got hurt in crossing by one
of the oxen All our men have been on duty except Knight in the morning. Made 7
miles Encamped on the bank of the river near to where we crossed. Grass wood &
water plenty. The men were much exposed in fording the river. The horse teams
are the best in fording streams when bottom is firm. The bottom of this stream
is quicksand. It will not do to stop in the current. The water will work the
sand from under your team untill the water will be to deep for the catle to
work, Some ox teams double their teams. We turned in single team. Would have
crossed without difficulty only two of our teams missed the ford some. We then
gave them more team to extricate them Was done without any of the wagons took in
water to wet any of goods. Before we entered the stream we hoisted the beds of
the wagons 5 or 6 inches A tremendious thunder storm with rain and some hail
near sunset

T.17th Cloudy morning. Jackson better Knight worse. The men on gaurd in the fore
part of the night could not find the camp Stayed out untill daylight Distant
thunder in the afternoon Some rain. The road was sandy and part muggy Made 22
miles Encamped in prairie No wood Plenty of grass and water Intented to seek the
timber. Last nights rain swelled a creek so much that we could not cross

W.18th Stormy night & this morning Two miles from our last night encampment we
came to Prairie Creek which was 8 feet deep in the chanel We fixed two wagon
beds Lashed them together in which made a boat to ferry in. It done well It
carried the loading in each wagon at al load and the empty wagon at a load We
got all our wagons and loading over in good order Loaded them and starded again

Met other streams on our route which were also rather deep to ford By raising
the wagons beds up we forded them without much damage to our loading, At Prairie
Creek there were a great many emigrants No less then four different ferries In
opperations Encamped In prairie with no wood or buffolo cheeps The men have to
take a cold supper Grass plenty

Th 19th. Clear White frost. Ferried wood creek In our wagon beds. At those
ferries there Is some stealing going on unless you use great care. Some of our
crowd lost a revolver, some a sack of flour. We lost some of our dried beef this
day the revolver was discoverd and obtained and also at the same tent a sack of
flour with mark used by those that lost same, but the person that had It denied
taken It and claimed It on the same plan that the looser did. This flour was
bought at Kanesville In sacks with the merchant mark and no other.

 F. 20 Cool clear morning A part of the road this day was wet and heavy Made 15
miles Encamped In prairie Wood scarse Water and grass plenty Last night Joseph
Wells stayed at our encampment He was In search of an ox that strayed off
the previous night Wells Is about a day journey ahead of us We heard this day
that George Perkins Is about the same. Last night one of Mrs Walkers work ox
strayed. Enoch went In search of him, Found him Some of the company saw for
several days some elk and antelopes. We have seen for several days the heads of
bufaloes or rather the skulls, but no live once

S.21st Clear morning. At noon we came to Platte River For the first time the
road was excellent to Platte from our last nights encampment. Wells and George
Perkins came to our encampment In the evening Made 13 miles Warm day wind south
Thunder & rain In the night with modorate wind

DIARY OF THE OREGON TRAIL TOUR

KEN AND LAURA JONES(continued)

SEPTEMBER 7, 1995 – THURSDAY

The weather, with a windy chilly morning and a temperature of fifty degrees, has changed to cloudy rain threatening skies. We are off on the trail at 9:00 am. The road made ninety-degree turns north and west, most of the way, to coincide with the section corners. Since it was not platted, the pioneers did not have to worry with this, but generally followed the Platte River. We crossed the trail frequently. Our first stop was the Plum Creek Cemetery. This is a burial place for a small wagon train of emigrants who were attacked by Indians on August 5, 1864. Eleven men were killed. Our lunch break required us to drive, off the main road, along a private lane for about a quarter of a mile. We parked our rigs in a circle surrounded by farm buildings and equipment. One of the buildings was the restored Gilman's stage station, later to become the Midway Pony Express Station. Back on the road after lunch, we stopped at the Fort McPherson Monument, originally called Cottonwood Springs. A fort was built there to accommodate the emigrants. A short distance farther, we passed a National Veterans Cemetery, with rows of white headstones surrounded by well maintained lawn and landscaping. Our next stop required parking all of our sixteen R. V.'s along the road side, blocking one lane of our two lane road! From here we hiked up a steep trail to the Sioux Lookout Monument. We climbed about four hundred feet in elevation, to a bluff, where the monument was located. What a view we had! We were back in an hour, with no complaints for blocking the road. As we head west on I-80 to Ogallala, we note the corn and soy bean fields have turned to pasture, with bales of hay dotting the landscape. We camp for the night at Meyer Campground. The grounds are grassy, with many trees. We will be here through tomorrow, and have changed our clocks to Mountain Time, one hour earlier. After a camp social, we all have a meat loaf dinner at the Country Kitchen restaurant in Ogallala. Ogallala is located about twenty miles east and a little north of the northeast corner of Colorado. From here the Oregon Trail heads northwest, bypassing Colorado, on its way to Scotts Bluff. Our elevation here at Ogallala is 3214 feet, 2000 feet higher than our starting point in Independence. Although the terrain is still basically flat, we see mountains in the distance.

Nathaniel Myer Diary

S 22nd Cloudy and windy morning Had a bad road Number sloughs and some small creeks all being swollen by the rain that fell last night Made 22 miles Encampment for the night a wet situation We left one of our best Illinoise heiffers, being lame, at the place where we stoped at noon Wells & Perkins left us in the morning We saw several buffaloe heads with the skins on them

M.23d Clear morning Sines of boffaloe Seen none of the animels yet Upon examining some of the guides we are about 244 miles from the Missourie River Made 20 miles Encamped Buffolo chips to cook

T.24th Clear morning Buffalo chips will answer for fuel when wood is not to be had. Made 20 miles Camped near the river Grass, wood scarse, Water supply plenty About 4 o, clk pm. came to the river where the bluffs came to the river Also sand deep Was heavy hawling nearly the whole way since we came to the river

W 25th Raine last night and in the morning nearly all day Made 20 miles Camped on the bank of the Platte a few miles east of the last timber for 200 miles. Passed two excellent springs at the foot of bluff

Th.26th Cloudy all day Camped near Bluff Creek. Made 20 miles, Bad roads for the larger part

F. 27th Cloudy all day Crossed Bluff Creek Beautiful clear stream 5 rods wide 2 feet deep. Low banks, quicksand bottom, Sandy road in the forenoon The afternoon not as sandy Made 22 miles Camped where water and grass are plenty, Wood we have brought with us, We passed some beautiful springs of clear water

S 28th Rained last night Cloudy at sunrise Clear a part of the day Thunder gust approaching Made 12 miles Camped Grass & Water good Brush and buffolo chips for fuel. Yoked two cows this morning in the room of a yoke of oxen They worked tolarably well Rained and wind blowed a good gale part of the night

S. 29th Clear morning. This morning we left our spring wagon or rather brock it to pieces Took the wood for fuel and left the iron. Mother and myself are to sleep in an ox wagon I drove the two black mares to last nights camp. We are now by Horns Guide 372 miles from the Missourie River Made 18 miles Camped close to the river. Grass fair The two previous days seen some few buffalos at a distance

DIARY OF THE OREGON TRAIL TOUR
KEN AND LAURA JONES(continued)

SEPTEMBER 8, 1995 – FRIDAY

This is a "free day". we are up at 6:00 am for an early morning clothes wash
at the laundry here at Meyer Campground. After Laura is through with this chore,
I served up our breakfast omelet, with polenta, ham, and toast. the Myer train
women would have washed their dusty, grimy garments with the cold, muddy water
of the Platte River, and then cooked mush, with bacon, over a fire of buffalo
chips! While Laura cleaned the dishes, I unhooked our pickup from the trailer.
Off to town, we stopped at an anique mall, where Laura purchased a set of
glasses that match some we have at home. After a visit to the Ogallala post
office to mail some letters (including checks for our third-quarter tax
estimates!), we found a "Radio Shack" to obtain a needed outside antenna for our
C.B. radio. After lunch at "A Little Bit of Heaven", we stocked up with
provisions at Safeway, gassed up at Texaco, and returned to camp. Following a
camp social, we are on our own for dinner; a delicious "Steak Diane", with all
the trimmings! Nathaniel Myer does not mention Ogallala in his diary, but
my guess is that the Myer train camped here May 22, 1853. They had been on the
trail for over two months, while this is our fifth day of travel!

SEPTEMBER 9, 1995 – SATURDAY

After our morning briefing, we broke camp and headed west at 9:00a.m.
Traveling along fields of newly-planted wheat, some corn, and soy beans, our
first stop was Ash Hollow and Windlass Hill. We parked our R. V.'s along the
highway, and boarded selected motor homes for the short drive to the trail head.
Here, as we climbed Windlass Hill we viewed deep wagon tracks coming down the
steep hill to the hollow below. From the top of the hill we enjoyed a vista

Figure 10   Windlass Hill

Figure 11   Sioux Lookout - East of Ogallala

37

Figure 12

Jail Rock

Figure 13
Courthouse Rock

Figure 14
Chimney Rock

in all directions. Due to the precipitous terrain, the emigrants found this area to be one of the most dangerous, and difficult parts of the Oregon Trail. Nathaniel Myer, in his diary entry of may 30th., mentioned "bad and heavy roads". I wondered if he was referring to Ash Hollow?

Back on the road, we pass the town of Lewellen, mentioned in Nathaniel Myer's diary, as a reference point of their night's stop on the Oregon Trail. Next, we arrived at a little town called Oshkosh, where we surrounded their city park for lunch. Both the town and park were neat and tidy. With a population of under eight hundred, Oshkosh impressed us with its amenities, including a free swimming pool! Laura and I visited with one of the residents, who gave us an insight about the hopes and struggles that they were facing.

We have been gradually gaining altitude, and now are at 3400 feet. Court house rock, and Jail rock are outcroppings along the trail that stand out for miles. Our group again boarded the same motorhomes to travel closer to the trail head. The wind was blowing gusts of sand that stung our faces. The interesting formations were landmarks that the emigrants could see several days before reaching them. As we traveled west toward Chimney Rock, we passed some very nice homes on prosperous farms. We also noted oil wells, which could be the reason for the nice homes! We reach the Chimney Rock Visitor Center, where we watched an interesting movie concerning the importance of Chimney Rock to the pioneers. Like Court House and Jail Rocks, it was a formation that could be seen a couple of days before reaching the area. It probably was the most mentioned landmark found in pioneer diaries. Nathaniel Myer mentioned "Camped three miles east of Chimney Rock" in his diary entry of June 1, 1853. We concluded our day's journey at a camp outside Bayard, called The Oregon Trail Wagon Train. It truly is a camp, on the trail,used by the emigrants. As the camp R. V. area is small, our rigs are cramped, with little room between. The area is grassy and covered with large shade trees. For dinner, we were treated to a barbeque of huge steaks cooked to our liking, with doggie bags for the left overs. We will make good use of them as we continue our journey. After dinner, we sat around a campfire for a songfest. This is one of the few campfires that we have had on this trip. The evening was cool, and, without a moon, the stars sparkled in the dark sky. I thought that this could be the same camp mentioned in Nathaniel Myer's diary. The trip is more exciting to us, knowing that Laura's ancestors' footsteps, mile after mile along this trail, are now retraced by us.

M.30th Rained last night Cloudy at sunrise Clear in the afternoon We left the old Durham bull. Could not travel further. Wells & Perkins met us in the fore part of the day Wells was hunting catle, His whole stock had run off the last night Enoch and Fruit went with him John was looking at the old bull which was back about 5 miles back from camp. Found Wells catle that had not been found before. Wells is in advance about 5 or 6 miles Made 16 miles Camped 3/4 mile from the river. Had bad and heavy roads Crossed Castle River Beautiful clear stream Quicksand botom 8 rods wide 18 inches deep Good crossing

T.31st Cloudy at sunrise Hail storm between 3 & 5 o clock pm Some ofthe hail stones as large as hens eggs No perticular damage sustained Made 20 miles camped. Good grass Water 1 mile fromcamp

W June 1st Cloudy & some rain. Some of the calfs feet are giving out. The boys are doctering them at noon Made 25 miles Road good Camped 3 miles east of chimny rock 440 miles west of the Missourie.

DIARY OF THE OREGON TRAIL TOUR
KEN AND LAURA JONES(continued)

SEPTEMBER 10, 1995 – SUNDAY

Today is the shortest traveling day so far; twenty-seven miles! We have been
rotating from front to back each day. Would you believe today was our day to be
number one! Tomorrow we will be last, eating everyones dust! Oh well!! Here at
the Oregon Trail camp we are served a huge camp breakfast consisting of bacon,
sausage, pancakes, and french toast, topped off with delicious camp coffee
brewed over the campfire, and served in tin cups! We arrive at our camp(a
shopping center parking lot in Scottsbluff!) around 11 am. The lot has electric
power poles, but after we all hook up, the circuit breaker blew, leaving
us totally self-contained. After lunch in our R. V.'s, we spent the rest of the
day at Scotts Bluff National Monument. This is the highlight of our trip so far.
We see wagon trails, take in the visitor center, and ascend, in our vehicles, to
the top of the bluff. Here we have panoramic views of irrigated fields, making
"patchwork quilts" of the valley below. For some reason, Nathaniel Myer does not
mention Scottsbluff,though they had to pass this way. In his diary for
Thursday, June 3rd, he writes, "Rained last night. Made 20 miles. Camped near
river. Grass poor, oxen tired. We had a thunderstorm, with wind and rain."
Perhaps the clouds of the storm obscured the bluff.

Scottsbluff is located on Highway #26, about twenty miles east of the
Wyoming border. The North Platte River separates the city from the town of
Gering. With a combined population exceeding 22,000, the area is the hub of
business and agricultural activity in western Nebraska. The elevation here is
3880 feet. Today, Joe and Reta celebrated common birthdays. Joe turned 85,while
Reta has reached the unbelievable age of 90! They are as active as most of us

42

Figure 15

Scottsbluff, Nebraska

Figure 16
Overlooking the
Landscape

Figure 17

Oregon Trail Wagon Train
Camp - Bayard, Neb.

43

"youngsters", and join in hikes, etc., with much enthusiasm. They are an inspiration to us all!

SEPTEMBER 11, 1995 – MONDAY

This is another short-traveling day of seventy-seven miles to Guernsey, Wyoming, but with much to see. Due to these two short days, Laura and I were allowed to continue at the head of the line! The weather cooperated in the early morning, with sunshine, while we prepared our rigs for travel, and had our briefing for the day. We had thunderstorms last night. Enroute to "Stuart Campsite", we encountered another thunderstorm, after which the day became sunny and mild. Capt. Stuart, a fur trapper for John Jacob Astor, established a camp, just across the border of Nebraska, in Wyoming, during the winter of 1812. Due to the weather, he stayed here until spring. He actually created much of the routing for the Oregon Trail, having traveled this way from, Astoria, Oregon to St. Louis, Missouri.

From "Stuart Campsite", we traveled on to Lingle, Wyoming for a great breakfast at the Stagecoach Cafe. Their specialty is biscuits and gravy, which I really enjoyed. On to Fort Laramie for a two-hour visit, including lunch in our R. V.'s. Fort Laramie grounds are quite large, with many of the old buildings restored. We were able to go inside most of them, and found the rooms furnished with items of that period(1840–90). The parade ground, and surrounding areas, were landscaped with manicured lawns, and shade trees. We questioned that it looked that elegant during the fort's active years. Our camp for the night was at Larson Park, outside of Guernsey, Wyoming. Located along the Platte River, the park is very picturesque, with grass and shade trees. Included is a public golf course, but, unfortunately, our time did not allow for a round of golf. Some of the golfers, however, stopped to chat. After unhooking our pickup, we took a side trip, with the rest of the group. First we stopped to view wagon

Figure 18

Stuart Campsite

Figure 19

Fort Laramie

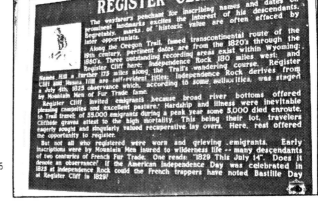

Figure 20

Register Cliff

45

ruts cut through a limestone outcropping, that were quite deep. We wondered how the emigrants accomplished that. Next, we drove to register cliff, famous for pioneer names carved in the soft limestone rock. The trail passed by here, making it convenient for name and date carving. This was done, not only by the emigrants, but by recent visitors as well. Some of the cliff is fenced to protect the history of this rock. We looked for Laura's ancesters without success. It was like hunting for a needle in a haystack! I did find the name K Jones 1840! Nathaniel Myer mentioned coming near Fort Laramie, and traveling through the rough trail of the Black Hills(now called Laramie Mountains). Their camp the night of June 5th had to be in this vicinity.

SEPTEMBER 12, 1995 – TUESDAY

Having left larson park at 9:00am, we found ourselves at the rear of the caravan. No dust though, as we traveled on paved roads on our way to Alcova Reservoir. Our first stop was for refueling in a little town called Douglas, Wyoming. With only one station available, it was quite a slow process, and, since we were at the back of the line, we were last! When we were finally through, Laura asked the station operator what he was going to do to celebrate his good fortune. He replied "I am going to close up, and go fishing!"

The weather was warm and sunny all day. Antelope can be seen frequently, grazing the fields, like cattle, along I-25, as we drove toward casper. The terrain is hilly, and mostly covered with native grass. Our lunch break found us winding down a narrow road to Ayres Natural Bridge Park. The little park is quite picturesque, with manicured grass, lots of large trees, and surrounded by red rock cliffs. Laprele Creek divides the park. A foot bridge gave us a good vantage point for viewing the natural bridge formed by years of erosion. Some of our group climbed on top of the arch, as it is not very high. Laura and I remember visiting this pretty park, on one of our earlier trips, many years ago.

46

Back on the Interstate, we headed for Casper, where we stopped at a shopping center for provisions. Our camp was along the shore of nearby Alcova Reservoir. Those of our group that had large rigs, feared problems with negotiating the steep access road to the lake shore. All made it safely, but worried about getting back out tomorrow! We had no facilities, but we were located within a few feet of this pretty lake. It would make a good picture for an R. V. Sale promotion! After getting situated, a few of us took a little side trip to see the canyon where water backed up from the Alcova Dam. Boats were coming out from the upper reaches of the canyon, after a day of fishing. It surely looked inviting!

Nathaniel Myer mentioned passing two trading stations along our day's route. One, probably, was Fort Caspar, but I am not sure about the other.

Figure 21   Sunrise - Alcova Lake
West of Casper, WY

Figure 22   Ayres Natural Bridge, WY

NATHANIEL MYER DIARY(continued)

Th 2nd cloudy at sunrise Clear in the afternoon Made 20 miles Part of the road
heavy Camped near the river Grass midling Fruit sold one work for $100. Storm
approaching about sunset

F.3rd Rained last night Cloudy & windy from the west Made 20 miles Camped near
to the river Grass poor Oxen tired Thretening rain at sunset

S.4th. Rained last night Cloudy at sunrise Thunder and rain about noon Made 22
miles Camped near the river. Grass poor saw some small trees on the north side
of the river Cool all day For several days we saw a few Indians

S 5th. Cloudy morning. Rained last night. Franklin stood gard the fore part of
the night. Got lost Staid out until daylight 12 m. oposite Fort Laramie a number
of Indians came to where we stoped at noon on horseback. They have mocosinse and
tried buffoloe meet to sell or barter for bread etc etc seen some of wells' They
are 3 miles west of us Passed Perkins camp seen Laramies Peak The top covered
with snow Made 23 miles and camped Grass poor. We passed several Indian
villiges. One of Enocks two horse wagon wheel tire brok He fixed it up with hoop
iron for the present

M.6th clear morning. All day. Yesterday afternoon and this day we traveled on
the Black Hills. Rough and hilly road made 18 miles. Camped near a fine runing
stream. Wood plenty Grass poor

T 7th. Clear and warm day. Road good Thunder & rain between 5 & 7 o clock pm
Made 22 miles Most of the distance the road was good Camped near the Platte
River Wood scarce Grass midling

W 8th Clear morning Thunder and few drops of rain in the afternoon Had some good
and very bad road Camped on high ground Wild sage for fuel No water with a mile
Wells brock an axel tree of one of his wagons came back about six miles Found

one or rather found a wagon that was left which answered his purpose and Enock found a wheel off the same wagon that answered his broken wheel

Th 9th Clear morning Thunder High wind Light rain Made 20 miles Camped Wood scarse Water 1/2 mile of Grass midling

F.10th Wind blowed down all the tents last night. Made 21 miles Part of the road sandy and heavy Camped close to the river. Wood, water and grass plenty We passed a tent in which a still babe was born The mother was doing well

S.11th Clear and beautiful morning. Thunder near sunset No rain Made 18 miles Camped on the bluff Brought the water with us. Sage for fuel Grass poor Campment all round us Passed two trading places The road sandy and heavy the most of the distance. Sold one our our work oxen at $18 He got lame

DIARY OF THE OREGON TRAIL TOUR

KEN AND LAURA JONES(continued)

SEPTEMBER 13, 1995 – WEDNESDAY

I took a picture of a beautiful sunrise over Alcova Lake, but because of the lack of sufficient daylight, it may not come out. Since our caravan was spread out along the lake shore, our briefing for today's journey was received on our C.B.'s. Those who were worried about negotiating the steep climb from the lake shore to the road above, had no problems. We were on our way by 8:45 a.m.

Independence Rock, our first stop today, is another landmark of the Oregon Trail. Again, we found lots of carvings, but with the rock composed of hard granite, the carving was difficult. A few of the more agile, and adventuresome souls of our group scrambled up the steep, smooth slope of the bluff to the top. I wondered if any of the pioneers had the energy, and the desire to climb it! Independence Rock, supposedly, was named by some Oregon Trail travelers, who arrived here on the 4th of July!

Further on the Oregon Trail, we arrived at Devil's Gate, and Tom Sun Ranch. Nathaniel Myer wrote in his diary on June 14, 1853: "Camped near the Devils Gate, A curiosity indeed. A branch of Sweetwater passes through a small gap of rock, which are between three and four hundrd feet. I was mistaken in saying that a branch of Sweetwater passed through the gate. The whole river passes through. We were realy in a salaratus rigion. The women gathered gallons of it, apparently as pure as that that is sold in market in the States." There is a monument here, dedicated "To the pioneers buried here on the Tom Sun Ranch. 1830 – 1870. Ezra Meeker often visited this spot". The scenery here is awesome.

Traveling on west, our lunch break was taken at Split Rock, another landmark of the trail. The formation is named from its opening, splitting the rock. It is

51

marvelous how well these historic sites have been preserved and monumented.

After another one station fuel stop, Laura read, over the C.B. radio, from the Myer diary entries covering this area. He mentioned camping a few miles west of Ice Springs. As we passed by here, we were informed that the Oregon Trail travelers stopped at nearby Ice Slough, where they could find ice, year around. Our group enjoys the diary; especially when it relates to places that we are now visiting.

Our traveling portion of the day ended at a rustic trailer park outside of Lander, Wyoming. The park has a number of buildings taken from a nearby ghost town. One of them housed our group for a roast beef dinner. We are now at an elevation of 5357 feet.

Figure 23
Independence Rock

Figure 24
Devil's Gate

Figure 25
Split Rock

53

A PIONEER WAGON TRAIN

NATHANIEL MYER DIARY(continued)

S.12th clear morning made 25 miles had no water for the stock from in the morning until we camped. Plenty of water Sage fuel. Good grass

M.13th. Clear morning A snow bank about 1/2 miles on our rout Franklin went to it Brought some to train Treaded the company with it Saw Wells They were all well About 7 miles west of us his train G. Perkins is in with Wells' train Made 14 miles Camped on Greasewood Creek Plenty of water Grass and fuel scarse The men have the whole stock about a mile from camp

T.14th Clear and cool morning The women washed some cloths in the evening This morning they are froze stif Crossed Sweetwater River on a bridge Paid $3. per wagon Swam the loose horsses and catle Camped near the Devils Gate A curiosity indeed A branch of Sweetwater passes through a small cap of rock which are between three and four hundrd feet I was mistaken in saying that a branch of Sweetwater passed through the gate The whole river passes through. We where realy in a salaratus rigion The women gather gallons of it apparently as pure as that that is sold in market in the States We passed Independence rock

W 15th Clear morning In crossing a small branch tollys wagon turned over herself and children in it. George M was nearly smothered with water mud and other things. Good many of her bed and other clothing got wet and mudy One of the wagon wheels considerable injured Detained about three hours Made 16 miles Camped near a fine stream of water about a mile left of the main road Plenty of water and sage. Grass poor

Th 16th Clear morning Passed Stone Bluff and Cottenwood Creek Fine clear swift stream 12 feet wide 3 inches deep Made 17 miles Camped some distance from the water Stock has no water Grass poor Sage for fuel Water we brought with us from the river about 5 miles

F 17th Clear yesterday Cortez bought a wagen and a yoke of oxen. We leave the

old wagn. Fruit exchanged wagens also We started early and stoped at 10 1/2 o
clock am at the river untill 3 o clock pm During this time we swam all the stock
across the river and back again the pasture being better on the other side The
women and men washed cloth etc Made 18 miles Camped a few miles west of the Ice
Springs Grass poor No water but was brought with us I had none to wash myself
Sage scarse

S.18th Clear morning At noon some of the men went about 3/4 mile to the left of
road and brought several bukets full of snow in We passed two springs within six
feet of each other The one warm The other cool Snow banks on both side of the
road I went to one of them It was 5 to 10 feet deep Made 20 miles Camped near a
snow bank which afords water for stock and cooking Grass fair

SEPTEMBER 14, 1995 - THURSDAY

We broke camp at 8:00 am, an hour earlier than our usual time, and headed west on Highway #28. We "crawled" up a six percent grade, that lasted for miles, until we reached the summit at an elevation of 8,200 feet! Here we stopped to allow everyone to catch up. Benny and Irene had transmission problems with their van. At South Pass, we parked in an area that barely held all of our rigs. From here, we traveled, in five vehicles, about twelve miles, to the actual Oregon Trail crossing of the Continental Divide. The elevation at this point was 7,400 feet. We found a monument, placed by Ezra Meeker, stating "The Oregon Trail, 1843-1857" Traveling west, we began passing some cultivated fields, with cattle grazing. Lunch, at Farson, Wyoming, consisted of buffalo burgers, and french fries. Around the corner, we topped lunch with huge ice cream cones! Stet, who is very slim, could not resist the jumbo size, consisting of four large scoops, with cones on top and bottom!

On our way again, we entered open range, with signs, along the roadway, advising this. One cute sign read "Antelope entering highway at 55 mph"! We crossed the Green River, headed for I-80. Since the freeway was involved in a construction project, we took a parallel highway to Little America, which is a huge truck stop, restaurant, gift shop, and motel. After much confusion, our rigs were refueled, and an hour later, we were headed for Lyman, Wyoming, our stop for the night. The Myer diary mentions South Pass, and the Green River. They did not have a problem crossing South Pass, but the Green River was a different story. His diary entry of June 25th describes the crossing: "Rapid stream. We succeeded well in swimming the catle across it." Then, on June 26th.,

Figure 26   South Pass

Figure 27   K-Bar Ranch campground
Lander, WY.

he writes "The wagon mother and I sleep in was taken over at near sunrise, we being with it. The second wagon was one of Walkers. The boat broke loose from the main line; boat and wagon floated down the river some distance; lodged on an island. Boat and wagon was brought back all save. One of the ferrymen left the boat, took water, and was drowned".

SEPTEMBER 15, 1995 – FRIDAY

After breakfast in our trailer, consisting of cold cereal topped with sliced bananas, melon, toast, and coffee, we skipped the morning briefing, to refill our propane tanks. I can imagine how the pioneers would enjoy having gas stoves, furnaces, and hot water! The closest propane dealer was in Mountain View, about eight miles south. We caught up with our caravan at Fort Bridger, which originally was Jim Bridger's Trading Post, and then became a military post. We were able to visit many restored buildings, and particularly enjoyed a duplication of the old Bridger Trading Post, now housing a rustic gift shop. At the picnic area outside the fort, our wagonmasters treated us to coffee, iced tea, and a variety of donuts. Benny and Irene continued to have transmission problems. After traveling west from Fort Bridger, their van finally "gave out" at a town called Kemmerer, Wyoming. Incidentally, this was the location of the first J.C. Penney store. Fortunately, the town has a Ford garage that can get them going again. We left them there, with the hope that they can catch up with us soon. We are traveling at elevations above 6,000 feet, and temperatures exceeding eighty degrees. For the most part the landscape is barren hills, with mountains in the distance. Close to towns the land is cultivated, with fields of livestock. The land seems to be productive if it has water. We stopped for groceries, gas, and the night's camp, at Montpelier, Idaho. Laura continues to read the Myer diary, covering the area we traveled, to our appreciative group. His diary entry of July 4th indicates they camped along Bear River, probably at,

FORDING A RIVER

58b

Figure 28 Ft. Bridger

Figure 29 Ft. Bridger Trading Post

what now is, Montpelier. It would appear that they were ahead of schedule, as most Oregon Trail travelers hoped to be at Independence Rock by this date. Montpelier, one of Idaho's oldest towns, was established by Brigham Young and his Mormon followers. Located at the junction of Highway #89 and #30N, we are at an elevation of around 6,900 feet. Highway #30 generally follows the Oregon Trail through Montpelier.

NATHANIEL MYER DIARY(continued)

S.19th Clear morning Distant thunder A few drops of rain Made 22 miles Camped Snow 1 mile of No other water Grass poor 5 miles east of the summit of the Rocky Mountain

M.20th Clear morning Crossed the summit of the Rocky Mountain. Yesterday it was 2 weeks that we saw snow for the first time and every day since Camped. No water for stock. Grass poor Fuel scarse. Water for cooking brought with us

T.21st Clear morning Wind west blowing a strong gale all day Crossed ietle Sandy Rapid stream 4 feet deep Camped not far from it Grass poor Sage for fuel The road good Equal to any pike I ever saw

W.22nd Clear and cold morning The men are all tressed with their blanket coats Made 10 miles Camped on the bank of Big Sandy. To deep to ford. We are waiting until morning and then determine what to do. To ford or ferry

TH 23rd Clear. Froze the water in the pools Forded the creek without much difficulties by proping up the wagon beds therewere not any of the goods wetted Made 10 miles Camped a short distance from Big Sandy Grass still poor Sage for fuel Water we brought with us where we forded the creek in the morning

F 24th Clear cool morning Three of Walkers men on the sick list Temperance and Menervi sick Made 16 miles. Camped five miles east of Green River. Had no water for our stock since yesterday at 10 o,clock am. Grass poor Sage for fuel Water for cooking brought with us

S. 25th Clear morning Six miles brought us to Green River Rapid stream We succeeded well in swiming the catle across it We only lost two or three yearling calfs We were not two hours in swiming all over Others have been two or three days at it and lost a number of them The horsses troubled us a good teal Wells & Perkins are hear with their trains The wind to strong to ferry wagons. Some expectations of getting our wagons over near sunset They ferrymen began to take wagons over but there being so many to take across before our turn came that the first of our wagons was taken over near the rise of the sun

S 26th Clear and beautifull morning The wagon that mother and myself sleep in was taken over at near sunrise we being with it The second wagon was one of Walkers. The boat broke loose from the main line. Boat and wagon floated down the river some distance Lodged on an island. Boat and wagon was brought back all save. One of the ferrymen left the boat Took water and was drowned. An emigrant died here yesterday he is to be enterred the day I attended the funeral A sermon was delivered from a paptist preacher Was appropriate and suitable Wells and Perkins left here about four o clk pm. After dark we got all the wagons across the river

M 27th Cloudy stormy morning With considerable difficulties the women got breakfast This was one of the stormies days we have had on the jouney Snowed several times Made 8 miles Camped Water sage and grass plenty

T.28th Clear came morning. White frost Wells & Perkins camped in sight Made 16 miles Camped Water sage grass fair Walkers turned a wagon over not much damage Snow seen on both sides of the road Some banks not far of the road

W.29th Cloudy morning Rained last night The road this day was steep acent and decent, stony, with many ravine and chuck holes One of our best wagons the fore axel brock. Snow all the way on our right Some close to the road Made 17 miles

61

Camped Water some distance off Grass poor. A part of some of our ox teams got scared Run a short distance. No injury sustained. Franklin fixed the broken axel How it will do is to be tested

Th 30th Clear and pleasant morning White frost The first 4 miles was rough and hilly Forded Hams Fork Bad crossing Got all the wagon accross save Descended a long and steep hill Became alevated above some of the banks of snow considerably. At noon we had snow at the dinner which was brought a short distance to where we stoped. Grass was good The axel that Vranklin fixed went last evening Went about 14 miles this day then failed intirely. Franklin at noon went back to get a wagon if he could. Mother, one driver and myself stayed with the wagon The rest of the teams and catle went on to the place of encampment for the night which was about three miles. The broken wagon with it load was brought to camp at dark. Franklin got no wagon He got a part of an axel & some bands with which he is fixing it again

JULY F.1st Clear morning Thunder & rain last night This day a part of the road was steep ascents & decents Stony Made 26 miles Camped near Smith Fork Water sage and grass good Yesterday Crooks left us George Perkins lodged with us

S.2nd Clear morning Crossed Smith Fork and a small branch which where bridged At the former paid two dollars At the other ten cents per wagon The whole stock went free Perkins left us at noon He was in search of two cows Did not find them In the afternoon crossed Thomas Creek on a bridge Paid $25 for the whole train Camped in the botom of said creek Grass & water good Willows for fuel Made 20 miles Had good roads

S.3rd. Clear morning Some fog The first seen west of the Missourie Had steep ascent and desent the first 8 miles Made 12 miles Camped some distance from the river Wood & water scarse Grass good

M 4th. Clear morning We had to make use of an ox yoke for fuel this morning This was a sumer day. Made 20 miles. Camped to the left of the road on Bear River

Grass good, Fuel sage, Crossed several fine streams none of them bad to cross

DIARY OF THE OREGON TRAIL TOUR

KEN AND LAURA JONES(continued)

SEPTEMBER 16, 1995 – SATURDAY

After an R. V. breakfast, we were heading northwest on Highway #30 to Soda Springs, which was an emigrant camp, and is now a nice little town. Soda Springs is a geyser that erupts every hour, spewing soda water over a flat rocky area. The hard mineral water has stained the rock an orange–brown color. Unfortunately, the geyser did not erupt while we were there. From Soda Springs, we headed west to Fort Hall Replica. By now we have shed our jackets, needed for the early morning chill, as the weather is very warm and sunny. The fields are cultivated with potatoes, grain, and sugar beets. We are following the Snake River, which provides irrigation for these crops. There are some harvested wheat fields that are getting a drink from the big sprinkler systems. Our group from Minnesota suggested that there is alfalfa planted under the corn. We had not run into that before. Since Fort Hall is only a memory, a replica has been built. I thought a fort was a military installation, but in this case, it was a trading post, eventually operated by the Hudson Bay Company. Here, the Indians and trappers would exchange furs for provisions etc. The fort was built in 1834, and was abandoned in 1858.

We drove on to Fort Hall Indian Reservation for a lunch stop at an Indian trading post. The buffalo stew, we ordered, was mostly vegetables, and served with Indian bread. A large clothing store and gift shop occupied the balance of our lunch time.

After lunch, we stopped at Massacre Rocks State Park. This area has some well-preserved wagon ruts remaining from thousands of wagons passing by, on their way to Oregon and california. On August 9, 1862, a band of disgruntled

Indians massacred a small wagon train of emigrants, trapped here. We continued our days journey, west to Raft River Crossing, where the Myer train left the Oregon Trail. In his diary entry of July 12th, Nathaniel Myer mentions crossing the east, middle, and west branches of Raft River. They were now on the California trail, which will intersect the Applegate Trail at Winnemucca, Nevada; then, on the Applegate trail, to their destination, Ashland, Oregon. In the diary of an ealier emigrant, Joel Palmer, dated August 8,1845, while at Fort Hall, he writes: "Great efforts were made to induce the emigrants to pursue the route to California. The most extravagant tales were related, respecting the dangers that waited a trip to Oregon." In as much as our group will be continuing on the Oregon Trail, I intend to make reference to the Palmer diary, as he traveled this same route. Upon conclusion of the diary covering our tour, I will return to the Myer diary, covering the remainder of their journey to Ashland.

We camped for the night at Declo, Idaho, at a very nice park, with grass and trees, along the Snake River.

SEPTEMBER 17, 1995 – SUNDAY

This is a rest day at our Declo R. V. park. Last night we were treated to a barbeque ribs and chicken dinner, followed by an Oregon Trail movie; very nice evening. At the restaurant here, Laura and I joined John and Patty for an omelete breakfast, which was delicious. After breakfast, we drove around the country side, through Declo, Burley, and Rupert. The farms around here seem prosperous, with nice homes. We were told that this area is in a "banana belt", with relatively mild winters. It should be a nice place to live, and raise a family. After stops at Smith's market, Walmart, and a Chevron gas station, we returned to our park for lunch. Because I was getting rather "shaggy", Laura gave me a haircut after lunch. Looking at photographs of the pioneer men, I

65

doubted that they bothered with haircuts or shaving! I then enjoyed a football game, on our R. V. Color TV set, between San Francisco and New England. Again, I thought of the emigrants, and reflected that it would be nice if they could have enjoyed such a luxurious day of rest. Perhaps, in their own way, they did. We completed the warm and sunny day by barbequing steaks for dinner.

SEPTEMBER 18, 1995 – MONDAY

Our caravan headed west, after an R. V. breakfast, with the first stop at Stricker Store. The store was built in 1865, and is the oldest building still in existence, on the Oregon Trail, in Idaho. Stricker built his home close by, around 1900. Someone, from the Oregon Trail Society, opened the house for us to tour. I was reminded of my grandparents' home in Central Point, Oregon. The setting here is delightful, with prosperous farms abundant. I would imagine that it was a nice stopping point for the pioneers, and later the stagecoach travelers.

Our next stop was Shoshone Falls, which was a highlight for all of us. It reminded us of Niagra Falls; not as large, but similar in shape. We had an R. V. lunch in Twin Falls, at Smith's parking lot, and then traveled on to One Thousand Springs. There is a pretty park here, along the Snake River, which accommodated all of our rigs. Across the river are high bluffs, with many waterfalls cascading down to the river below. The falls come from an underground river that is believed to originate around the Craters Of The Moon area. The emigrants traveled along this area, but higher up on the ridge. Occasional ruts are visible. Our camp is at the Three Island Crossing State Park, located at the pioneer crossing of the Snake River. The park is very nice, with shade trees and lawn. Since the electricity has been turned off for repairs, and there is no sewer hookup, we are self-contained, except for water. Tonight we had an outdoor potluck picnic, with lots of great food.

Figure 30 Shoshone Falls, ID

Figure 31

Stricker Store

Figure 32   1000 Springs, SD

67

In Joel Palmer's diary entry of August 23, 1845, he writes about crossing the Snake River, at Three Island Crossing: "The difficulties attending the crossing of this stream had been represented as being almost insurmountable; but upon examination we found it an exaggeration. From the main shore to first island there is no difficulty; from first island to second, turn well up, until nearly across, then bear down to where the road enters it. The water is not deep until nearly across, and not then if you keep well up stream. From second island to main shore is more diccicult; it is about three hundred yards wide and the current very rapid. Strike in, heading well up for two rods, then quartering a little down until eight or ten rods from shore; then quartering a little up for fifteen or twenty rods; then strike up for the coming out place; the bottom is gravelly. With the exception of a few holes, the water for the first fifteen rods is the deepest part of the ford. The bottom is very uneven; there are holes found of six or eight feet in width, many of them swimming. Those crossing this stream can excape the deepest of these holes by having horsemen in the van and at each side; it is necessary that there be attached to each wagon four or six yoke of oxen, the current being swift; and in the passage of these holes, previously alluded to, when one yoke is compelled to swim, the others may be in shallow water. Great care must be taken that these teams be not beat down too low and pass over the ripple; and to prevent such a casualty, two drivers must attend each wagon. Before attempting the passage of the river all articles liable to damage, from coming in contact with the water, should be piled on the top of the wagon bed. We commenced crossing at eleven o'clock, a.m., and at one o'clock p.m., we effected the passage of the stream, and were so fortunate as to land our goods free from all damage."

SEPTEMBER 19, 1995 - TUESDAY

We have a relative long traveling day to Vale, Oregon. It's a beautiful day; sunny, with many cultivated fields across the Idaho farm belt. Our first stop is about 25 miles east of Boise at a hill called Bonneville Point, named for a french captain. Captain Bonneville, when reaching this view point in 1833, exclaimed: "Le Bois!", a phrase used by trappers and explorers in reference to what is now known as the Boise valley. Ruts are visible heading down the hill towards Boise. After Bonneville Point, we entered freeway I-84, traveling west though Boise, exiting at Garden City for fuel and lunch. Back on the trail, we stopped at the Ward Massacre Site. a monument here states: "On August 20, 1854, near this spot, Alexander Ward's 20 member party, which was Oregon bound, was attacked by Indians. Only two young boys survived the attack. Military retaliation for the slaughter, resulted in the hanging of three Indians, determined to have participated in the murders, also near this spot."

Traveling on towards Vale, we arrived at Keeney Pass. The trail ruts here are plainly visible, as the trail ascends the pass, named after Jonathan Keeney, a fur trader and one time partner of Jim Bridger. Keeney operated a ferry on the Snake River at Fort Boise. In the fall of 1863, he built a wayside at the present site of Vale. This log cabin povided a place for travelers to rest. The cabin was later replaced with a stone house, which is still in existence in Vale. We reached our camp, in Vale, about 4:00 pm. After securing our rigs, we were pleased to have Benny and Irene join us at our usual evening social. They had traveled, today, all the way from Salt Lake City, where they had rented a car. Their vehicle was still being repaired. Since there was no reasonable way for them to tow their trailer, still in Kemmerer, they will stay in nearby lodging facilities. After another delicious dinner, downtown, we enjoyed a walk by some business buildings decorated with large murals, depicting various Oregon

Trail wagon train scenes. Ice cream cones secured at a local confectionery store, provided us with a treat, as we walked backed to camp.

Joel Palmer's diary entry of September 2, 1845 describes the Boise area: "We reached Fort Bois. This is a trading post of the Hudson's Bay Company, established upon the northern side of Snake or Lewis River, and one mile below the mouth of Bois River. This fort was erected for the purpose of recruiting, or as an intermediate post, more than as a trading point. It is built of the same materials, and modeled after Fort Hall, but is of a small compass. Portions of the bottoms around it afford grazing; but, in a general view, the surrounding country is barren. North of this fort is an extensive plain, which has an extremely unfertile appearance; but, I am informed, that during the winter and spring months it affords good grazing. At this fort they have a quantity of flour in store, brought from Oregon City, for which they demanded tweny dollard per cwt., in cash; a few of our company being in extreme want, were obliged to purchase at this exorbitant price. At this place the road crossed the river; the ford is about four hundred yards below the fort, and strikes across to the head of an island, then bears to the left to the southern bank; the water is quite deep, but not rapid; it swam some of our smallest work cattle; the bottom is solid and smooth. We cut poles, and laid them across the top of our wagon-beds, piling our loading on them; answering a twofold purpose—preventing our loading from damage, and also by its weight keeping the wagons steady and guarding them against floating. In about three hours we effected our passage in safety, but few of the goods getting wet. We went up the bottom a half mile, and there encamped; driving our cattle on an island hard by, to graze. Fort Bois is about two hundred and eighty miles below Fort Hall, following the wagon road; but by crossing the river at Fort Hall, and going down on the north side the distance would be lessened, as the river bears off south, and then north; and judging from the appearance of the country, I think a road may be found, equal, if not better than the one on the south side; and, I doubt not, the grazing will be found better."

SEPTEMBER 20, 1995 – WEDNESDAY

Another beautiful, sunny day greets us, as we travel along the trail to Baker City. The valley of Vale and Ontario is lush, with irrigated fields of onions. We began climbing into arid mountains, and then down to the last view of the Snake River, at Farewell Bend State Park. Here, we stop for a thirty-minute break at this delightful spot of grass and trees along the river.

Upon leaving Farewell Bend, we followed a county road along Burnt Creek, through a little town called Huntington. The Oregon Trail was particularily difficult along this section, as it crossed Burnt Creek frequently. Back on I-84, we traveled west to Baker City. Here we visited the Flagstaff Hill Interpretive Center. Looking out of the big picture windows of the building, we enjoyed a marvelous view of the valley, with wagon ruts in the foreground, and the Blue Mountains in the distance. This is, perhaps, the best interpretive center on the Oregon Trail, though all of them are well done. We spent most of the afternoon wandering through the exhibits of life along the trail. Laura and I enjoyed a live theatre presentation, depicting life during those migrating years. This has been a highlight of our trip. The fact that we were here last year made our visit, today, the "frosting on the cake".

Tonight, we enjoyed a ham dinner at the VFW hall in Baker City; another great meal. One of the women that volunteered for serving us, was, also, a volunteer at the interpretive center!

Joel Palmer, in his diary entries of September 6th and 7th, described his experiences along Burnt River: September 6. "We made about twelve miles. The road is up Burt River, and the most difficult road we have encountered since we started. The difficulties arise from the frequent crossings of the creek, which is crooked, narrow and stony. We were often compelled to follow the road, in its windings for some distance, over high, sidelong and stony ridges, and frequently through thickets of brush. The stream is about ten or twelve yards in width, and is generally rapid. The hills are high, and covered with grass."

September 7. "This day we traveled about twelve miles. The road exceeded in roughness that of yesterday. Sometimes it pursued its course along the bottom of the creek, at other times it wound its way along the sides of the mountains, so sidelong as to require the weight of two or more men of the upper side of the wagons to preserve their equilibrium. The creek and road are so enclosed by the high mountains, as to afford but little room to pass along, rendering it in some places almost impassable. Many of the mountains viewed from here seem almost perpendicular, and of course present a barren surface. The eye is occasionally relieved by a few scrubby cedars; but along the creek is found birch, bitter cottonwood, alder, etc., in quantity, and several kinds of brush and briars, so inpenetrable as to preclude ingress. The road pursues its course through these thickets, the axe having been employed; but it is so very narrow as almost to prevent travel. A little digging, and the use of the axe, united with the erection of bridges would make this a very good road. At first view this road appeared to us impassable, and so difficult of travel, as almost to deter us from the attempt; but knowing that those who had preceded us had surmounted the difficullties, encouraged us to persevere. It required much carefulness, and the exercise of skill on the part of our drivers to pass along and avoid the danger of the way. We pursued our route without any loss, with the exception of that attending the breakage of two wagon tongues, done in crossing some deep ravines. We also experienced difficulty in finding our cattle, which had strayed away. Five miles from camp the road turns up a spring branch to the right, which we

followed two miles, crossing it very frequently; it then turns up the mountain
to the left, until it strikes another ravine. We followed up this for one mile,
where water makes it appearance. Here is found a good camp, one mile to running
water. This portion of the road is solid and of good travel."

SEPTEMBER 21, 1995 – THURSDAY

It was a chilly morning in Baker City, with the temperature near freezing,
but by afternoon it warmed to near eighty degrees. We headed northwest on I-84
climbing towards the Blue Mountains. The fields between Baker City and LaGrande
are mostly irrigated, with grain, alfalfa, and cattle prevelent. Up into the
pine forest of the Blue Mountains, we stopped at Blue Mountain crossing
interpretive center, operated by the Forest Service. Normally closed this time
of year, the ranger opened the facility, and gave us a guided tour. The trail
here is quite visible, with ruts and tracks through the pine forest. This
section, and on to Pendleton, was the most difficult portion of the Oregon Trail
so far. There are three trails covering one and one-half miles. Brochures were
given to us, to take on the hike. We were all impressed! The descent down
"Cabbage Hill", on old Highway #30, was spectacular! We had views of the fields
of wheat as far as the eye could see. Unfortunately, the road was steep, and
full of pot holes that threatened our rigs. Chuck and Virgene suffered a broken
hitch on their trailer, which required them to stay in Pendleton for repairs.

Our caravan traveled on, without Chuck and Virgene, through miles of wheat
fields. As we entered the little town of Echo, we heard the voice of a local law
officer, on our C.B.'s, asking City Hall if they were expecting a bunch of R.
V.'s! Upon receiving an answer of no, he replied " Well, you've got fifteen or
twenty headed your way"! After parking our rigs all over the little town, we
were welcomed by a city official, who gave us brochures of Fort Henrietta, and
Oregon Trail sites around Echo. We are a curiosity wherever we go!

Figure 33
Farewell Bend

Figure 34

Ore.Trail Interpretive Ctr

Figure 35
Blue Mountain crossi
Interpretive Ctr

74

Our camp for the night is at the Krebs ranch at Cecil, Oregon, where we parked our rigs in driveways and the barn yard. Wagon ruts of the Oregon Trail still remain through this remote, but picturesque country. All that remains of the town is an old building that once housed the Cecil store and post office. The Krebs family treated us to an outdoor barbeque of lamb kabobs, beans, and potato salad, followed with homemade pies!

Joel Palmer writes about crossing the Blue Mountains in his diary entries: "September 14. This day we traveled about ten miles. The road ascended the mountain for one and a half or two miles, then wound along the ridge crossing many deep ravines, and pursuing its route over high craggy rocks; sometimes directing its course over an open plain, at others through thick groves of timber, winding among fallen trees and logs, by which the road encumbered. The scenery is grand and beautiful, and cannot be surpassed; the country to a great distance is rough in the extreme. It may strictly be termed a timber country, although many small prairies are dotted over its surface. The valleys are beautiful and the soil presents a very rich appearance. We encamped in an opening, on the south side of a range of mountains running to the north, and found water in plenty in the bottom of the ravine, on our left, about one fourth of a mile from the road. The timber growing in this region is principally yellow pine, spruce, balsam, fir, and hemlock; among the bushes I noticed laurel. September 15. This day we traveled about nine miles, over the main ridge of the Blue Mountains. It is mostly a timbered country through which we passed; the scenery is delightful, resembling in grandeur that presented on yesterday's travel. We had a fine view of the Cascade Mountains to the west. Mount Hood, the loftiest of these, was plain to the view. It was some one hundred and fifty miles distant and being covered with snow, appeared as a white cloud rising above those surrounding it. To the north of Mount Hood, and north of the

Columbia is seen Mount Saint Helen. We halted for the night at Lee's encampment."

It would appear, from later diary entries, that Palmer followed a route north of ours, to Umatilla, and then along the Columbia, to The Dalles.

SEPTEMBER 22, 1995 – FRIDAY

We woke up to a chilly morning, with the temperature around freezing. In spite of a dry camp, we enjoyed a breakfast of ham and eggs, with cornbread left over from lunch at a restaurant in Pendleton. Immediately after leaving the Krebs ranch we traveled on a dusty, washboard road to a monument on Four Mile Canyon. Ruts on the trail here are quite noticeable. The fields of wheat were all around us, contoured to coincide with the rolling hills. We were all glad when we hit pavement again. Our next stop was at Arlington for a coffee break, where, at a local restaurant, Laura had a doughnut, and I had apple pie, with ice cream! There was no sign of Chuck and Virgene, so they, hopefully, will catch up with us at Biggs. Our caravan entered the freeway here at Arlington, and headed west, along the Columbia River to The Dalles. As we traveled west,the landscape along the river gradually changed from brown to green. At Biggs Junction, we stopped for gas, and had an R. V. lunch in a parking lot overlooking the Columbia. Chuck and Virgene, having made repairs, caught up with us here. Bob and Louise, who live in Yakima, Washington, left the caravan, at Biggs, to return home. Bob, who is planning a hip replacement, was in much discomfort from his aching hip. With my bad knees, I can certainly relate to his condition! We visited the old Court House in The Dalles, where the curator (dressed in pioneer clothes) told us interesting stories about the early day times. She was so cute in her attire that I could not resist taking her picture! We ended our traveling day at Memaloose State Park, on the river, west of The Dalles. Russ and Rita brought some excellent homemade wine to our evening

Figure 36
Krebs Ranch - Cecil, OR.

Figure 37
Wilma Ransom-Storyteller
Old courthouse, The Dalles
OR.

Figure 38
Rowena Crest- Columbia R.
Overlook

social. That seemed to loosen up the group for some good joke telling! For dinner, Laura and I ate some of our "leftovers", as we enjoyed the river view through the "dining room" window of our trailer. Lots of river shipping was evident. The weather continues to be warm and sunny.

Palmer's party arrived at The Dalles on September 29th. He writes: "This day we traveled about five miles, which brought us to The Dalles, or Methodist Missions. Here was the end of our road, as no wagons had ever gone below this place. We found some sixty families in waiting for a passage down the river; and as there were but two small boats running to the Cascade Falls, our prospect for a speedy passage was not overly flattering."

SEPTEMBER 23, 1995 – SATURDAY

Our briefing this morning was a half-hour earlier, and we were on the road at 8:30 a.m. for a big day. Our first stop was an overlook of the Columbia River. We could see a little town on the Washington side, and lots of boats, with fishermen, on the river below. It was so picturesque, that I took several photos. We, then, stopped at The Dalles for groceries at an Albertson's store. We left most of our R. V. 's in the parking lot, while we visited the Fort Dalles Museum. Here, there are two restored homes that we toured, as well as a couple of buildings, housing antique vehicles and wagons. On our way to The Dalles, earlier today, we passed many orchards of apricots, cherries, and apples. On one of The Dalles streets, there is a large rock, called Pulpit Rock, which Jason Lee used for his sermons to the Indians.

Leaving The Dalles, we drove on Highway #197, through rolling hills of grain, to Tygh Valley. We parked our rigs beside the road at Dufur for lunch. As we looked out of our "dining room" window, we had a great view of Mt. Hood. Our caravan headed for the Cascade Mountains, following the old Barlow Road that caused the emigrants much misery, and peril, traversing the steep rocky grades.

We "dry camped" in a meadow at the edge of the forest, at the foot of Mt. Hood. After a hike on the Barlow Trail for about a mile down through the thick forest, we took another walk to an old pioneer grave site. The day ended with a caravan supper of hot dogs, salads, and desserts. The night is chilly, after a warm, sunny day. Our elevation is over 4,000 feet. Joel Palmer spent the month of October, helping to find, and build a route that became the Barlow Trail. His diary, covering this period is agonizing and fascinating. Beginning on September 30th., he writes: "This day we intended to make arrangements for our passage down the river, but we found upon inquiry, that the two boats spoken of were engaged for at least ten days, and that their charges were exorbitant, and would probably absorb what little we had left to pay our way to Oregon City. We then determined to make a trip over the mountains, and made inquiries respecting its practicability of some Indians, but could learn nothing definite, excepting that grass, timber and water would be found in abundance; we finally ascertained that a Mr. Barlow and Mr. Nighton had, with the same object, penetrated some twenty or twenty-five miles into the interior, and found it impracticable. Nighton had returned, but Barlow was yet in the mountains, endeavoring to force a passage; they had been absent six days, with seven wagons in their train, intending to go as far as they could, and if found to be impracticable, to return and go down the river. We succeeded in persuading fifteen families to accompany us in our trip over the mountains, and immediately made preparations for our march. On the afternoon of the first of October, our preparations were announced as complete, and we took up our line of march; others in the mean time had joined us, and should we fall in with Barlow, our train would consist of some thirty wagons." October 3. "This morning I started on horseback in advance of the company, accompanied by one of its members. Our course led us south over a rolling, grassy plain; portions of the road were very stony. After a travel of fourteen miles, we arrived at a long and steep declivity, which we descended, and after crossing the creek at its base ascended a bluff; in the bottom are seen several small enclosures; where the Indians have cultivated the soil; a few Indian huts may be seen along this stream. Meek's company crossed Deshute's River near the mouth of this stream, which is five miles distant. After ascending, we turned to the right, directing our course over a level grassy plain for some five miles or more, when we crossed a running branch; five miles brought us to stony branch, and to scattering yellow pine timber. Here we found Barlow's company of seven wagons. Barlow was absent at the time, having with three others started into the mountain two days before. We remained with them all night."

OCTOBER 5. At an early hour this morning, I proceeded down the mountain to the stream at its base. I found the descent very abrupt and difficult; the distance was one-half mile. The water was running very rapid; it had the same appearance as the water of the Missouri, being filled with white sand. I followed this stream up for some distance, and ascertained that its source was in Mount Hood; and from the appearance of the banks, it seems that its water swell during the night, overflowing its banks, and subside again by day; it empties into Deshute's River, having a sandy bottom of from two rods to half a mile wide, covered with scrubby pines, and sometimes a slough of alder bushes, with a little grass and rushes. We then ascended the mountain, and as our stock of provisions was barely sufficient to last us through the day, it was found necessary to return to camp. We retraced our steps to where we had struck the bluff, and followed down a short distance where we found the mountain of sufficiently gradual descent to admit of the passage of teams; we could then follow up the bottom towards Mount Hood, and as we supposed that this peak was the dividing ridge we had reasonable grounds to hope that we could get through. We then took our trail in the direction of the camp; and late in the evening, tired and hungry, we arrived at Rock Creek where we found our company encamped. Barlow had not yet returned, but we resolved to push forward.

OCTOBER 6. We remained in camp. As the grazing was poor in the timber, and our loose cattle much trouble to us, we determined to send a party with them to the settlement. The Indians had informed us that there was a trail to the north, which ran over Mount Hood, and thence to Oregon City. This party was to proceed up one of the ridges until they struck this trail, and follow it to the settlement. Two families decided upon going with this party, and as I expected to have no further use for my horse, I sent him with them. They were to procure provisions and assistance, and meet us on the way. We had forwarded, by a company of cattle-drivers from The Dalles, which started for the settlement on the first of the month, a request that they would send us provisions and assistance; but as we knew nothing of their whereabouts, we had little hope of being benefited by them. The day was spent in making the necessary arrangements for the cattle-drivers, and for working the road. In the afternoon, Barlow and his party returned. They had taken nearly the same route that we had; they had followed up the bluff to this branch of the Deshutes, to within twelve or fifteen miles of Mount Hood, where they supposed they had seen Willamette Valley. They had then taken the Indian trail spoken of, and followed it to one of the ridges leading down to the River Deshutes; this they followed, and came out near our camp. We now jointly adopted measure for the presecution of the work before us.

OCTOBER 7. Early in the morning, the party designated to drive our loose cattle made their arrangements, and left us. And as we supposed our stock of provisions was insufficient to supply us until these men returned, we dispatched a few men to The Dalles for a beef and some wheat; after which we divided our company so as that a portion were to remain and take charge of the camp. A sufficient number were to pack provisions, and the remainder were to be engaged in opening the road. All being ready, each one entered upon the duty assigned him with an alacrity and willingness that showed a full determination to prosecute it to completion, if possible. On the evening of the 10th, we had opened a road to the top of the mountain which we were to descend to the branch of the Deshutes. The side of the mountain was covered with a species of laurel bush, and so thick, that it was almost impossible to pass through it, and as it was very dry we set it on fire. We passed down and encamped on the creek, and during the night the fire had nearly cleared the road on the side of the mountain. On the morning of October 11, a consultation was had, when it was determined that Mr. Barlow, Mr. Lock, and myself, should go in advance, and ascertain whether we could find a passage over the main dividing ridge. In the mean time, the remainder of the party were to open the road up the creek bottom as far as they could, or until our return. We took some provision in our pockets, an axe, and one rifle, and started. We followed up this branch about fifteen miles, when we reached a creek, coming in from the left. We followed up this for a short distance, and then struck across to the main fork; and in doing so, we came into a cedar swamp, so covered with heavy timber and brush that it was almost impossible to get through it. We were at least one hour in traveling half a mile. We struck the opening along the other fork, traveled up this about eight miles, and struck the Indian trail spoken of before, near where it comes down the mountain. The last eight miles of our course had been nearly north—a high mountain putting down between the branch and main fork. Where we struck the trail, it turned west into a wide, sandy and stony plain, of several miles in width, extending up to Mount Hood, about seven or eight miles distant, and in plain view. I had never before looked upon a sight so nobly grand. we had previously seen only the top of it, but now we had a view of the whole mountain. No pen can give an adequate description of this scene. The bottom which we were ascending, had a rise of about three feet to the rod. A perfect mass of rock and gravel had been washed down from the mountain. In one part of the bottom was standing a grove of trees, the top of which could be seen; from appearance, the surface had been filled up seventy-five or eighty feet about them. The water came tumbling down, through a little channel, in torrents. Near the upper end of the bottom, the mountains upon either side narrowed in until they left a deep chasm or gulf, where it emerged form the rocky cliffs above. Stretching away to the south, was a range of mountain, which from the bottom appeared to be connected with the mountain on our left. It appeared to be covered with timber far up; then a space of over two miles covered with grass; then a space of more than a mile destitute of vegetation; then commenced the snow, and continued rising until the eye was pained in looking to the top. To our right was a high range, which connected with Mount Hood, covered with timber. The timber near the snow was dead. We followed this trail for five or six miles, when it wound up a grassy ridge to the left – followed it up to where it connected with the main ridge; this we followed up a mile, when the grass disappeared, and we came to a ridge entirely destitute of vegetation. It appeared to be sand and gravel, or rather, decomposed material from sandstone crumbled to pieces. Before reaching this barren ridge, we met a party of those who had started with the loose cattle, hunting for some which had strayed off. They informed us that they had lost about one-third of their cattle, and were then encamped on the west side of Mount Hood. We determined to lodge with them, and took the trail over the mountain. In the mean time, the cattle-drovers had found a few head, and traveled with us to their camp. Soon after ascending and winding round this barren ridge, we crossed a ravine, one or two rods in width, upon the snow, which terminated a short distance below the trail, and extended to the top of

Mount Hood. We then went around the mountain for about two miles, crossing several strips of snow, until we came to a deep kanyon or gulf, cut out by the wash from the mountain above us. A precipitate cliff of rocks, at the head, prevented a passage around it. The hills were of the same material as that we had been traveling over, and were very steep. I judged the ravine to be three thousand feet deep. The manner of descending is to turn directly to the right, go zigzag for about one hundred yards, then turn short round, and go zigzag until you come under the place where you started from; then to the right and so on, until you reach the base. In the bottom is a rapid stream, filled with sand. After crossing, we ascended in the same manner, went round the point of a ridge, where we struck another ravine; the sides of this were covered with grass and whortleberry bushes. In this ravine we found the camp of our friends. We reached them about dark; the wind blew a gale, and it was quite cold.

OCTOBER 12. After taking some refreshment, we ascended the mountain, intending to head the deep ravine, in order to ascertain whether there was any gap in the mountain south of us, which would admit of a pass. From this peak, we overlooked the whole of the mountains. We followed up the grassy ridge for one mile and a half, when it became barren. My two friends began to lag behind, and show signs of fatigue; they finally stopped, and contended that we could not get around the head of the ravine, and that it was useless to attempt an ascent. But I was of a different opinion, and wished to go on. They consented, and followed for half a mile, when they sat down, and requested me to go up the ledge, and, if we could effect a passage up and round it, to give them a signal. I did so, and found that by climbing up a cliff of snow and ice, for about forty feet, but not so steep but that by getting upon one cliff, and cutting holes to stand in and hold on by, it could be ascended. I gave the signal, and they came up. In the meantime, I had cut and carved my way up the cliff, and when up to the top was forced to admit that it was something of an undertaking; but as I had arrived safely at the top of the cliff, I doubted not but they could accomplish the same task, and as my moccasins were worn out, and the soles of my feet exposed to the snow, I was disposed to be traveling, and so left them to get up the best way they could. After proceeding about one mile upon the snow, continually winding up, I began to despair of seeing my companions. I came to where a few detached pieces of rock had fallen from the ledge above and rolled down upon the ice and snow,(for the whole mass is more like ice than snow); I clambered upon one of these and waited half an hour. I then rolled stones down the mountain for half and hour; but as I could see nothing of my two friends, I began to suspect that they had gone back, and crossed in the trail. I then went round to the south-east side, continually ascending, and taking an observation of the country south, and was fully of the opinion that we could find a passage through. The waters of this deep ravine, and of numerous ravines to the north-west, as well as the south-west, form the heads of Big Sandy and Quicksand River, which empty into the Columbia, about twenty-five or thirty miles below the Cascade Falls. I could see down this stream some twelve or fifteen miles, where the view was obstructed by a high range coming round from the north-west side, connecting by a low gap with some of the spurs of this peak. All these streams were running through such deep chasms, that it was impossible to pass them with teams. To the south, were two ranges of mountains, connecting by a low gap with this peak, and winding round until they terminated near Big Sandy. I observed that a stream heading near the base of this peak and running south-east for several miles, there appeared to turn west. This I judged to be the headwaters of Clackamis, which empties into the Willamette, near Oregon City: but the view was hid by a high range of mountains putting down in that direction. A low gap seemed to connect this stream, or some other, heading in this high range, with the low bottoms immediately under the base of this peak. I was of the opinion that a pass might be found between this peak and the first range of mountains, by digging down some of the gravel hills; and if not, there would be a chance of passing between the first and second ranges through this gap to the branch of Clackamis; or, by taking some of the ranges of mountains and following them down, could reach the open ground near the Willamette, as there appeared to be spurs extending in that direction. I could also see a low gap in the direction from where we crossed the small branch, coming up the creek of the 11th, towards several small prairies south of us. It appeared, that if we could get a road opened to that place our cattle could range about these prairies until we could find a passage for the remainder of the way. The day was getting far advanced, and we had no provisions, save each of us a small biscuit; and knowing that we had at least twenty-five miles to travel, before reaching those working on the road, I hastened down the mountain. I had no difficulty in finding a passage down; but I saw some deep ravines and crevices in the ice which alarmed me, as I was compelled to travel over them. The snow and ice had melted underneath, and in many places had left but a thin shell upon the surface; some of them had fallen in and presented hideous looking caverns. I was soon out of danger, and upon the east side of the deep ravine I saw my two friends slowly winding their way up the mountain. They had gone to the foot of the ledge, and as they wore boots, and were much fatigued, they abandoned the trip, and returned down the mountain to the trail, where I joined them. We there rested a while, and struck our course for one of the prairies which we had seen from the mountain. On our way we came to a beautiul spring of water, surrounded with fine timber; the ground was covered with whortleberry bushes, and many of them hanging full of fruit, we halted, ate our biscuit, gathered berries, and then proceeded down the mountain. After traveling about ten miles, we reached the prairie. It was covered with grass, and was very wet. A red sediment of about two inches in depth covered the surface of the ground in the grass, such as is found around mineral springs. A beautiful clear stream of water was running through the prairie, in the south-east direction. We had seen a prairie about two miles further south, much larger than this, which we supposed to be dry. We now took our course for camp, intending to strike through the gap to the mouth of the small branch; but we failed in finding the right shute, and came out into the bottom, three miles above where we had first struck the cattle or Indian trail. We then took down the bottom, and arrived in camp about eleven o'clock at night; and although not often tired, I was willing to acknowledge that I was near being so. I certainly was hungry, and my condition was so much better than that of my two friends, that I could not murmur. Our party had worked the road up the small branch, where they were encamped. On the morning of the 13th of October we held a consultation, and determined upon the future movements of the company. The party designated to bring us provisions had performed that service; but the amount of our provisions was nearly exhausted, and many of the party had no means of procuring more. Some of them began to despair of getting through this season. Those left with the camp were unable to keep the cattle together, and a number of them had been lost. The Indians had stolen several horses, and a variety of mishaps occured, such as would necessarily follow from a company so long remaining in one position. They were now on a small creek, five miles from Stony Hill, which we called Camp Creek, and near the timber. It was impossible to keep more than one third of the men working at the road; the remainder were needed to attend the camp and pack provisions. It was determined to send a party and view out the road, through to the open country, near the mouth of Clackamas, whilst the others were to open the road as far as the big prairie; a number of sufficient to bring up the teams and loose cattle,(for a number of families with their cattle had joined since we left, and portions of our company did not send their loose cattle,) to a grassy prairie in this bottom, and near the mouth of this creek, as the time required to pack provisions to those working on the road would be saved. All being arranged, the next thing was to designate the persons to go ahead of the party, and if found practicable to return with provisions and help; or at all events to ascertain whether the route were practicable. It was determined that I should undertake this trip. I asked only one man to accompany me. We took our blankets, a limited supply of provisions, and one light axe, and at eight o'clock in the morning set out. I was satisfied that the creek which we were on, headed in the low gap, seen from Mount Hood; and the party were to open the road up to this branch. but as I was to precede them, I passed up this creek for about eight or ten miles, when I discovered the low gap, went though it, and at noon arrived at the wet prairie, which we had visited the day before. The route was practicable, but would require great labor to remove the timber, and cut out the underbrush. We halted at the creek and took some refreshment; we then struck for the low gap between the first range of mountains running west, and the base of Mount Hood, and traveled through swamps, small prairies, brush, and heavy timber for about twelve miles, when we found the labor necessary to open a wagon road in this direction, to be greater than we could possibly bestow upon it before the rainy season. We determined to try some other route, retraced our steps six or seven miles, and then bore to the right, around the base of the mountain, when we struck into an old Indian trail. This we followed for seven or eight miles through the gap I had seen from Mount Hood. It is a rolling bottom of about four or five miles in width, and extending from the base of Mount Hood south for ten or twelve miles. The trail wound around the mountain, but as its course was about that we wished to travel, we followed it until it ran out at the top of the mountain. We then took the ridge west, and traveled until dark;

but as the moon shone bright, and the timber was not very thick, we turned an angle down the mountain to the left, to procure water. We traveled about three miles, and struck upon a small running branch; this we followed, until owing to the darkness, we were compelled to encamp much fatigued, and somewhat disheartened.

OCTOBER 14. At daylight we were on the way. My moccasins, which the night before had received a pair of soles, in yesterday's tramp had given way and in traveling after night my feet had been badly snagged, so that I was in poor plight for walking; but as there was no alternatinve, we started down the mountain, and after traveling a few miles I felt quite well and was able to take the lead. We traveled about three miles, when we struck a large creek which had a very rapid current, over a stony bottom. I had hoped to find a bottom of sufficient width to admit of a wagon road, but after following down this stream six miles, I was satisfied that it would not do to attempt it this season. The weather, which had been entirely clear for months, had through the night began to cloud up; and in the morning the birds, squirrels, and every thing around, seemed to indicate the approach of a storm. I began for the first time to falter, and was at a stand to know what course to pursue. I had understood that the rainy season commenced in October, and that the streams rose to an alarming height, and I was sensible that if we crossed the branch of the Deschutes, which headed in Mount Hood, and the rainy season set in, we could not get back, and to get forward would be equally impossible; so that in either event starvation would be the result. And as I had been very active in inducing others to embark in the enterprise my conscience would not allow me to go on and thus endanger so many families. But to go back and state to them the difficulties to be encountered and the necessity of taking some other course, seemed to be my duty. I therefore resolved to return, and recommend selecting some suitble place for a permanent camp, build a cabin, put in such effects as we could not pack out, and leave our wagons and effects in the charge of some persons until we could return the next season, unincumber with our families and cattle, and finish the road;--or otherwise to return to The Dalles with our teams, where we could leave our baggage in charge of the missionaries, and then descend the Columbia. And when my mind was fully made up, we were not long in carrying it into execution. We accordingly ascended the mountain, as it was better traveling than in the bottom. The distance to the summit was about four miles, and the way was sometimes so steep as to render it necessary to pull up by the bushes. We then traveled east until we reached the eastern point of this mountain, and descended to the bottom, the base of which we had traversed the day before. We then struck for the trail, soon found it, and followed it until it led us to the southern end of the wet prairie. We then struck for the lower gap in the direction of the camp, crossed over and descended the branch to near its mouth, where we found four of our company clearing the road, the remainder having returned to Camp Creek for teams. But as we had traveled about fifty miles this day, I was unable to reach the camp.

OCTOBER 15. This morning we all started for camp, carrying with us our tools and provisions. We reached camp about two p.m. Many of our cattle could not be found, but before night nearly all were brought into camp. The whole matter was then laid before the company, when it was agreed that we should remove over to the bottom, near the small creek, and if the weather was unfavorable, leave our baggage and wagons, and pack out the families as soon as possible. But as some were out of provisions, it was important that a messenger should be sent on ahead for provisions, and horses to assist in packing out. Mr. Buffum, and lady, concluded to pack out what articles they could, and leave a man to take charge of the teams and cattle until he returned with other horses. He kindly furnished me with one of his horses to ride to the settlement. He also supplied the wife of Mr. Thompson with a horse. Mr. Barlow and Mr. Rector made a proposition to continue working the road until the party could go to and return from the valley; they agreeing to insure the safety of the wagons, if compelled to remain through the winter, by being paid a certain per cent upon the valuation. This proposition was thought reasonable by some, and it was partially agreed to. And as there were some who had no horses with which to pack out their families, they started on foot for the valley, designing to look out a road as they passed along. Some men in the mean time were to remain with the camp, which as above stated was to be removed to a small branch on Shutes' Fork; and those who intended pushing out at once, could follow up it to the Indian trail. This all being agreed upon, arrangements were made accordingly.

OCTOBER 16. The morning was lowering, with every indication of rain. Messrs. Barlow and Rector started on the trip. All hands were making arrangements for moving the camp. In the mean time Mr. Buffum and his lady, and Mrs. Thompson, were ready to start. I joined them, and we again set out for the settlement. We had traveled about two miles when it commenced raining, and continued raining slightly all day. We encamped on the bottom of Shutes Fork, near the small branch. It rained nearly all night.

On the morning of the 17th October after our horses had filled themselves we packed up and started. It was still raining. We followed up this bottom to the trail, and then pursued the trail over Mount Hood. Whilst going over this mountain the rain poured down in torrents, it was foggy, and very cold. We arrived at the deep ravine at about four p.m., and before we ascended the opposite bank it was dark; but we felt our way over the ridge, and round the point to the grassy run. Here was grazing for our tired horses, and we dismounted. Upon the side of the mountain, where were a few scattering trees, we

91

found some limbs and sticks, with which we succeeded in getting a little fire. We then found a few sticks and constructed a tent, covering it with blankets, which protected our baggage and the two women. Mr. Buffum and myself stood shivering in the rain around the fire, and when daylight appeared, it gave us an opportunity to look at each others' lank visages. Our horses were shivering with the cold, the rain had put out our fire, and it seemed as though every thing had combined to render us miserable. After driving our horses round a while, they commenced eating; but we had very little to eat, and were not troubled much in cooking it.

OCTOBER 18. as soon as our horses had satisfied themselves we packed up and ascended the mountain over the ridge, and for two miles winding around up and down over a rough surface covered with grass. The rain was falling in torrents, and it was so foggy that we could barely see the trail. We at length went down a ridge two miles, when we became bewildered in the thick bushes. the trail had entirely disappeared. We could go no farther. The two women sat upon their horses in the rain, whilst I went back to search for the right trail; Buffum endeavoring to make his way down the mountain. I rambled about two miles up the mountain, when I found the right trail, and immediately returned to inform them of it. Buffum had returned, and of course had not found the trail. We ascended the mountain to the trail when a breeze sprung up and cleared away the fog. We could then follow the trail. We soon saw a large band of cattle coming up the mountain, and in a short time met a party of men following them. They had started from The Dalles about eight days before, and encamped that night four or five miles below, and as it was a barren spot, their cattle had strayed to the mountain to get grass. But what was very gratifying, they informed up that a party of men from Oregon City, with provisions for our company had encamped with them, and were then at their camp. We hastened down the maountain, and in a few hours arrived at the camp. But imagine our feelings when we learned that those having provisions for us, had despaired of finding us, and having already been out longer than was expected, had returned to the settlement, carrying with them all the provisions, save what they had distributed to these men. We were wet, cold, and hungry, and would not be likely to overtake them. we prevailed upon one of the men whom we found at the camp, to mount one of our horses, and follow them. He was absent about ten minutes, when he returned and informed us that they were coming. They soon made their appearance. This revived us, and for a while we forgot that we were wet and cold. They had gone about six miles back, when some good spirit induced them to return to camp, and make one more effort to find us. The camp was half a mile from the creek, and we had nothing but two small coffee-pots, and a few tin cups, to carry water in; but this was trifling, as the rain was still pouring down upon us. We speedily made a good fire, and set to work making a tent, which we soon accomplished, and the two women prepared us a good supper of bread and coffee. It was a rainy night, but we were as comfortable as the circumstances would admit.

OCTOBER 19. After breakfst, the drivers left us; and as the party which had brought us provisions had been longer out than had been contemplated, Mr. Stewart and Mr. Gilmore wished to return. It was determined that Mr. Buffum, the two females, Mr. Stewart, and Mr. N. Gilmore, should go on to the settlement, and that Mr. C. Gilmore, and the Indian who had been sent along to assist in driving the horses, and myself, should hasten on with the provisions to the camp. We were soon on the way, and climbing up the mountain. The horses were heavily loaded, and in many places the mountain was very slippery, and of course we had great difficulty in getting along. It was still raining heavily, and the fog so thick that a person could not see more than fifteen feet around. We traveled about two miles up the mountain when we found that whilst it had been raining in the valley, it had been snowing on the mountain. The trail was so covered with snow that it was difficult to find it, and, to increase our difficulty, the Indian refused to go any farther. We showed him the whip, which increased his speed a little, but he soon forgot it, was very sulky, and would not assist in driving. We at length arrived at the deep ravine, here there was no snow, and we passed it without serious difficulty. Two of our packs coming off, and rolling down the hill, was the only serious trouble that we had. When we ascended the hill to the eastern side of the gulf, we found the snow much deeper than on the western side; besides, it had drifted, and rendered the passage over the strip of the old snow somewhat dangerous, as in many places the action of the water had melted the snow upon the under side and left a thin shell over the surface, and some places holes had melted through. We were in danger of falling into one of these pits. Coming to one of these ravines where the snow had drifted very much, I dismounted in order to pick a trail through, but before this was completed, our horses started down the bank. I had discovered two of these pits, and ran to head the horses and turn them; but my riding horse started to run, and went directly between the two pits; his weight jarred the crust loose, and it fell in, presenting a chasm of some twenty-five or thirty feet in depth, but the horse, being upon the run, made his way across the pit. The other horses, hearing the noise and seeing the pits before them, turned higher up, where the snow and ice were thicker, and all reached the opposite side in safety. Our Indian friend now stopped, and endeavored to turn the horses back, but two to one was uneven game, and it was played to his disadvangage; he wanted an additional blanket; this I promised him, and he consented to go on. We soon met two Indians, on their way from The Dalles to Oregon City; our Indian conversed with them awhile, and then informed us of his intention to return with them. Whilst parleying with him, a party of men from our camp came upon the mountain with their cattle, they had driven teams to the small branch of the Deshutes, twelve miles below the mountain, where they had left the families, and started out with their cattle before the stream should get too high to cross. Whilst we were conversing with these men, our Indian had succeeded in getting one loose horse, and the one which he was riding, so far from the bank of pack-horses that, in the fog, we could not see him, and he returned to the settlement with the two Indians we had just met. Our horses were very troublesome to drive, as they had ate nothing for thirty-six hours; but we succeeded in getting them over the snow, and down to the grassy ridge, where we stopped for the night. My friend Gilmore shouldered a bag of flour, carried it half a mile down the mountain to a running branch, opened the sack, poured in water, and mixed up bread. In the mean time, I had built a fire. We wrapped the dough around sticks and baked it before the fire, heated water in our tin cups and made a good dish of tea, and passed a very comfortable night. It had ceased raining before sunset, and the morning was clear and pleasant; we forgot the past and looked forward to a bright future.

OCTOBER 20. At 8 o'clock we packed up, took the trail down the mountain to the gravelly bottom, and then down the creek to the wagon-camp, which we reached at 3 p.m. And if we had not before forgotten our troubles, we certainly should have done so upon arriving at camp. Several families were entirely out of provisions, others were nearly so, and all were expecting to rely upon their poor famished cattle. True, this would have prevented starvation; but it would have been meagre diet, and there was no certainty of having cattle long, as there was but little grass. A happier set of beings I never saw, and thanks bestowed upon us by these families would have compensated for no little toil and hardship. They were supplied with an amount of provisions sufficient to last them until they could reach the settlements. After waiting one day, Mr. Gilmore left the camp for the settlement, taking with him three families; others started about the same time, and in a few days all but three families had departed. These were Mr. Barlow's, Mr. Rector's, and Mr. Caplinger's, all of whom had gone on to the settlement for horses. Ten men yet remained at camp, and, after selecting a suitable place for our wagon-yard, we erected a cabin for the use of those who were to remain through the winter, and to stow away such of our effects as we could not pack out. This being done, nothing remained but to await the return of those who had gone for pack horses. We improved the time in hunting and gathering berries, until the 25th, when four of us, loaded with heavy packs, started on foot for the valley of the Willamette. But before entering upon this trip, I will state by what means the timely assistance afforded us in the way of provisions was effected. The first party starting for the settlement from The Dalles, after we had determined to take the mountain route, carried the news to Oregon City that we were attempting a passage across the Cascade Mountains, and that we should need provisions. The good people of that place immediately raised by donation about eleven hundred pounds of flour, over one hundred pounds of sugar, some tea, etc., hired horses, and the Messrs. Gilmore and Mr. Stewart volunteered to bring these articles to us. The only expense we were asked to defray was the hire of the horses. They belonged to an Indian Chief, and of course he had to be paid. The hire was about forty dollars, which brought the flour to about four dollars per hundred, and there were about one thousand pounds when they arrived. Those who had the means paid at once, and those who were unable to pay gave their due bills. Many of the families constructed pack-saddles and put them on oxen, and in one instance a feather bed was folded up and put upon an ox; but the animal did not seem to like his load, and ran into the woods, scattering the feathers in every direction; he was finally secured, but not until the bed was ruined. In most cases the oxen performed well. In the afternoon of the 25th October, accompanied by Messrs. Creighton, Farewell, and Buckley, I again started to the valley. We had traveled but a short distance when we met Barlow and Rector, who had been to the settlement. They had some horses, and expected others in a short time. They had induced a few families whom they met near Mount Hood to return with them, and try their chance back to The Dalles; but after waiting one day, they concluded to try the mountain trip again. We traveled up the bottom to the trail, where we encamped; about this time it commenced raining, which continued through the night.

OCTOBER 26. This morning at eight o'clock, we were on the way. It was rainy, and disagreeable traveling. We followed the trail over the main part of the mountain, when we overtook several families, who had left us on the twenty-second. Two of the families had encamped the night before in the bottom of the deep ravine; night overtook them, and they were compelled to camp, without fuel, or grass for cattle or horses. Water they had in plenty, for it was pouring down upon them all the night. One of their horses broke loose, and getting to the provision sack, destroyed the whole contents. There were nine persons in the two families, four of them small children, and it was about eight miles to the nearest settlement. The children, as well as the grown people, were nearly barefoot, and poorly clad. Their names were Powell and Senters. Another family by the name of Hood, had succeeded in getting up the gravelly hill, and finding grass for their animals, and a little fuel, had shared their scanty supply with these two families, and when we overtook them they were all encamped near each other. We gave them about half of our provisions, and encamped near them. Mr. Hood kindly furnished us with a wagon cover, with which we constructed a tent, under which we rested for the night.

OCTOBER 27. The two families who had lost their provisions succeeded in finding a heifer that belonged to one of the companies traveling in advance of us. In rambling upon the rocky cliffs above the trail for grass, it had fallen down the ledge, and was so crippled as not to be able to travel. The owners had left it, and as the animal was in good condition, it was slaughtered and the meat cured. After traveling four miles through the fresh snow, (which had fallen about four inches deep during the night,) we came to where the trail turned down to the Sandy. We were glad to get out of the snow, as we wore moccasins, and the bottoms being worn off, our feet were exposed. Two miles brought us to where we left the Sandy, and near the place where we met the party with provisions; here we met Mr. Buffum, Mr. Lock, and a Mr. Smith, with fourteen pack–horses, going for effects to Fort Deposit–the name which we had given our wagon camp. The numerous herds of cattle which had passed along had so ate up the grass and bushes, that it was with great difficulty the horses could procure a sufficiency to sustain life. Among the rest, was a horse for me; and as I had a few articles at the fort, Mr. Buffum was to take the horse along and pack them out. Two of his horses were so starved as to be unable to climb the mountains, and we took them back with us. The weather by this time had cleared up; we separated, and each party took its way. A short distance below this, our trail united with one which started from The Dalles, runs north of Mount Hood, and until this season was the only trail traveled by the whites. we proceeded down the Sandy, crossing it several times, through thickets of spruce and alder, until we arrived at the forks, which were about fifteen miles from the base of Mount Hood. The bottom of the Sandy is similar to the branch of Deshutes which we ascended; but in most cases the gravel and stones are covered with moss; portions of it are entirely destitute of vegetation. The mountains are very high, and are mostly covered with timber. At a few points are ledges of grayish rock, but the greater part of the mountain is composed of sand and gravel; it is much cut up by deep ravines, or kanyons. The trail is sometimes very difficult to follow, on account of the brush and logs; about our camp are a few bunches of brakes, which the horses eat greedily. The stream coming in from the southeast is the one which I followed down on the 14th, and from appearance I came within five miles of the forks. The bottom in this vicinity is more than a mile wide, and is covered with spruce, hemlock, and alder, with a variety of small bushes.

October 28. We started early, and after having traveled several miles, found a patch of good grass, where we halted our horses for an hour. We then traveled on, crossing the Sandy three times. This is a rapid stream; the water is cold, and the bottom very stony. We made about fifteen or sixteen miles only, as we could not get our horses along faster. We struck into a road recently opened for the passage of wagons. Mr. Taylor, from Ohio, who had left our company with his family and cattle on the 7th, had arrived safely in the valley, and had procured a party of men and had sent them into the mountains to meet us at the crossing of Sandy. They had come up this far, and commenced cutting the road toward the settlements. After traveling this road five or six miles we came upon their camp, where we again found something to eat; our provisions having been all consumed. The road here runs through a flat or bottom of several miles in width, and extending ten or twelve miles down the Sandy; it bears towards the north, whilst the creek forms an elbow to the south. The soil is good, and it is covered with a very heavy growth of pine and white cedar timber. I saw some trees of white cedar that were seven feet in diameter, and at least one hundred and fifty feet high. I measured several old trees that had fallen, which were one hundred and eighty feet in length, and about six feet in diameter at the root. We passed some small prairies and several beautiful streams, which meandered through the timber. The ground lies sloping to the south, as it is on the north side of the creek. In the evening it commenced raining a little. We remained at this camp all night.

OCTOBER 29. This morning, after breakfast, we parted with our friends and pursued our way. We soon ascended a ridge which we followed for seven or eight miles, alternately prairie and fern openings. In these openings the timber is not large, but grows rather scrubby. There are numerous groves of beautiful pine timber, tall and straight. The soil is of a reddish cast, and very mellow, and I think would produce well. We came to the termination of this ridge and descended to the bottom, which has been killed by fire. From this ridge we could see several others, of a similar appearance, descending gradually towards the west. We here crossed the creek or river, which was deep and rapid; and as our horses were barely able to carry themselves, we were compelled to wade the stream. Buckly had been sick for several days, and not able to carry his pack, I now found it of some advantage in crossing the stream, as it assisted in keeping me erect. Buckly in attempting to wade across, had so far succeeded as to reach the middle of the stream, where he stopped, and was about giving way, when he was relieved by Farewell, a strong athletic yankee from the state of Maine. In crossing a small bottom, one of the horses fell; we were unable to raise him to his feet and were compelled to leave him. The other we succeeded in getting to the top of the hill, where we were also compelled to leave him. The former died, but the latter was taken in a few days after by those who were opening the road. After being relieved of the burthen of the two horses, we pushed forward on foot, as fast as Buckly's strength and our heavy packs would allow; and as it had been raining all day, our packs were of double their former weight. At dark we met a party of men who had been through with a drove of cattle, and were returning with pack horses for the three families who were yet at Fort Deposit. We encamped with them. After crossing the Sandy our course was south-west over a rolling and prairie country. The prairie, as well as the timber land, was covered with fern. The soil was of a reddish cast, and very mellow, as are all the ridges leading from the mountain to the Willamette or Columbia River. We traveled this day sixteen or seventeen miles.

OCTOBER 30. This morning was rainy as usual. Four miles brought us to the valley of the Clackamis, which was here five or six miles wide. The road was over a rolling country similar to that we passed over on yesterday. To the left of the trail we saw a house at the foot of the hill; we made for it, and found some of our friends who had started from camp with C. Gilmore. The claim was held by a man named McSwain. We tarried here until the morning of the 31st, when we again started for Oregon City. Our trail ran for five or six miles along the foot of the hill, through prairie and timber land. The soil looks good, but is rather inclined to gravel; numerous streams flow down from the high ground, which rises gradually to a rolling fern plain, such as we traveled over on the 28th, and 29th. We then continued upon the high ground seven or eight miles, alternately through timber and fern prairies. We then turned down to Clackamis bottom, which is here about one mile wide; this we followed down for three miles, when night overtook us, and we put up at Mr. Hatche's, having spent just one month in the Cascade Mountains.

NOVEMBER 1. This morning we left Hatche's and in two miles travel we reached the crossings of the Clackamis River. At this point it is one hundred and fifty yards wide, the banks of gentle descent, the water wending its way for the noble Columbia over a pebbly bottom. Here is a village of about twenty families, inhabited by the Clackamis Indians, who are few in number, apparently harmless, and caring for nothing more than a few fish, a little game, or such subsistance as is barely sufficient to support life. There are but two or three houses in the village; they are made by setting up side and centre posts in the ground, the latter being the highest, to receive a long pole to uphold puncheons split out of cedar which form the covering; the sides are enclosed with the same material, in an upright position. These puncheons are held to their places by leather thongs, fastened around them to the poles that lay upon the posts. After examining this little community, the remains of a once powerful and war-like people, we obtained the use of their canoes, crossed over the river, and after two miles further travel we reached a point that had long been a desired object; where we were to have rest and refreshment. We were now at the place destined at no distant period to be an important point in the commercial history of the Union--Oregon City. Passing through the timber that lies to the east of the city, we beheld Oregon and the falls of the Willamette at the same moment. We were so filled with gratitude that we had reached the settlements of the white man, and with admiration at the appearance of the large sheet of water rolling over the falls, that we stopped, and in this moment of happiness recounted our toils, in thought, with more rapidity than tongue can express or pen write. Here we hastily scanned over the distance traveled, from point to point, which we computed to be in miles as follows, viz: from Independence to Fort Laramie, 629 miles; from Fort Laramie to Fort Hall, 585 miles; and from Fort Hall to Fort Bois, 281 miles; from Fort Bois to The Dalles, 305 miles; from The Dalles to Oregon City,(by the wagon route south of Mount Hood,) 160 miles, making the total distance from Independence to Oregon City, 1960 miles. Actual measurement will vary the distances, most probably lessen them; and it is very certain, that by bridging the streams, the travel will be much shortened, by giving to it a more direct course, and upon ground equally favorable for good road."

This was the end of Joel Palmer's facinating diary. It left me wondering what happened after that! History tells us that the Barlow road was completed, and operated by Mr. Barlow, as a toll road for future emigrants. Did palmer return the next spring to complete the road? What happened to him after that? I have made a mental note to do some research on this.

Figure 39
Barlow Trail

Figure 40
Mt. Hood - Barlow Trail

Figure 41

Oregon City
Interpretive
Center

103

SEPTEMBER 24, 1995 - SUNDAY

The alarm startled us at 5:45 this morning. The trailer was cold! Since we had no hookups, we just "bundled up" with warm clothing. After cooking ham and eggs for breakfast on our gas range, we were warmed by the heat generated from this. Back on the trail by 8:30 a.m., we stopped shortly thereafter at Government Camp, a settlement with a ski facility. Most of our group left in three of our smaller RV's, to walk the Laurel Hill portion of the Barlow Road. This section was considered to be the worst and most dangerous on the entire Oregon Trail. We continued on to Eagle Creek School, where we stopped for a coffee break. The day being Sunday, school was not in session. From there, we traveled on "back roads", descending through the mountain forest, to Oregon City. The drive reminded me of Palmer's diary account of their last few days, coming out of the mountains, and arriving at Oregon City.

Our son and daughter-in-law, Steve and Marie, along with our grand children, Vanessa and Bryan, met us at the Oregon Trail Interpretive Center, in Oregon City. The theatre entrance depicts the loading platform of a freight warehouse, with large wooden boxes of merchandise situated, conveniently, for the seating of the visitors waiting for the next performance. This created an ideal setting for picture taking by Steve and Marie, using various cameras belonging to our group. The Interpretive Center, different from the others, has a host that talks about the Oregon Trail, using slides to illustrate. A second theatre presents a history of the Oregon Trail. The outside of the building forms two huge conestoga wagons. Our camp for the night took us west, into the center of the Willamette Valley, to the little village of St. Paul, Oregon. The county fairgrounds, where we "bivouacked", also was void of hookups. We were really "roughing" it, especially since it has been raining intermittently during the time we have been in the Willamette Valley! I keep reminding myself about the pioneers! Tonight, after a "rained out" happy hour, we were greeted by the mayor of St. Paul, who joined us for a salmon dinner. Tomorrow will bring our last day of travel by caravan. None of us want this to end!

SEPTEMBER 25, 1995 – MONDAY

Today we travel forty three miles, to our final camp, at Rickreall. Rain showers are occasionally occurring, just to remind us that we are in Oregon! Our first stop is at Champoeg State Park for viewing exhibits and a movie at the visitor center. Laura and I remember camping here last year. The grounds are picturesque, with large trees, and manicured lawns. Oregon has wonderful state parks, for camping, picnicing, and waysides. Almost all of the campgrounds have hookups, but the setting creates a "feeling" of a campsite in the forest. From Champoeg, we traveled south, through the pristine farm land of the Willamette Valley, to Willamette Mission State Park. Located along the Willamette River, the park is the original site of the Willamette Mission, established by Rev. Jason Lee in 1834. Our group was greeted by the park ranger, who gave us a walking tour, and explained the history and operation of the park. It is unusual, in that, due to its large area and fertile ground, there are commercial orchards, and other farming activities, located within the park. The ranger took us for a hike, through a walnut grove, to the river. At this spot he pointed across the river to the site of the Mission, which was destroyed by the great flood of 1861. Our day, as well as our tour concluded at the Polk County Fairgrounds. A last happy hour was held in one of the fairground buildings, followed by a buffet dinner. After dinner, a program was held, in which each one of us received a "Rut Nut" diploma. The award declared: "On September 26, 1995, completed travel over the Oregon Trail from Independence, Missouri to the Willamette Valley in Oregon. Has endured heat and cold, wind and rain, dust and dirt, rough roads, bugs, flies, and other miserable conditions too numerous to mention. Has viewed and traveled miles of trails and swales, visited historic sites and studied geographical features enough to last a lifetime. This award gives the privilege of the most honorable title Rut Nut with all rights and benefits pertaining thereto." Our evening concluded with another video of the Oregon Trail.

SEPTEMBER 26, 1995 – TUESDAY

A farewell continental breakfast was served at the fairgrounds building at 8:30 a.m. Our wagonmasters, Russ and Rita, and our tailgunners, Vic, and Nancy, were presented gifts of appreciation for making this tour so special. We could not thank them enough, as our friends from Minnesota, Herb and Benny, acted as spokesmen for the group. It was now time to say goodbye, resolving that we would keep in touch, until we meet again. Though the memories will carry on, this journey, as all journeys must, has come to an end.

Now that we are through with the diary of our Oregon Trail journey, let's return to the Nathanial Myer diary. We left the Myer train, with Nathaniel's entry of July 4, 1853 stating that they were camped on Bear River.

T.5th Clear day Passed the Soda and Boiling Springs They are realy curiosities.
One of our cows died very suddenly this forenoon. Made 21 miles Camped 7 miles
west of the Fort Hall road Grass fair Sage for fuel No water for our stock and
none to cook with here We brought some with us from where we stopped at noon
There we had plenty of water but no grass Wells was with us at noon His train is
15 miles west of us

W 6th Clear morning The men had no water to wash themselves. We made about 9
miles to Cady's Creek where men and stock had water to their full satisfaction
which was about noon In the afternoon made 6 miles to Shoshonne Creek Beautiful
stream The most dangerous road to wagons of any we have come yet. We received no
injury There was a train before us who turned a wagon over and rolled down a
steep bank. What injury was sustained I am not able to say as I was ingaged in
helping our wagons when I saw the wreck Camped on Shoshonne Creek Grass fuel and
water good The girls gathered straberries

Th 7th Clear & cool morning Thunder but no rain Made 22 miles Camped on good
water. Grass fuel & water good A hilly road Some of the ascents & decents steep

F.8th Clear & cool at sunrise Made 14 miles in the forenoon to where there was
water fuel. Grass poor It is represented that there is no water for 25 miles
Near sunset we left our noon campment went 9 miles to the steep decent Fruit
undertook to take the teams down It Drove the foremost Did not advance far
Turned the wagon over The wagons and women stayed at sumit The stock was drove
down to good grass The men stayed with them no water for the stock

S.9th Clear Musketers bad We dcoondod tho steepest decent that we have met with
without any injury Great care was required Made 8 miles Found some water for men
and stock some short distance from the main road A noon halt. We did travel in

the afternoon Grass fuel & water good

S 10th Clear at sunrise For several days past It was warm from 8 a.m. To 6 p.m.
Made 18 miles Camped Grass fuel & water good

M.11th Clear day Made 14 miles gain 12 o clock M Camped for the night at Ford No
2 Sinking Creek. Grass good Water plenty In the branch Not of the best Fuel
scarse of every kind except willows They are poor excuse at any time when green.
Women washed

T 12th Clear Some cooler Crossed east branch of Raft River Bad sloughs In its
vicinity Crossed the midle and west branch of Raft Rivers Made 27 miles Camped
on the west branch of Raft river at second ford. Snow banks close by The road
for the most part good

W.13th Clear Cortez took sick yesterday. Some better this day. He kept his bed
all day. Made 17 miles Camped Cedar Creek Grass fuel & water good Had good roads
except some of the streams where bad crossings. We crossed several the day.
Cedar Creek a beautiful rapid clear stream

TH.14th Clear morning Made 15 miles Camped to the right of the road. Grass fuel
& water poor. Saw the curiosities of the pyramit circle It is realy delightful
to see the many pyramids of rock standing in a plain as they are. Cortez kept
his bed all day

F.15th Clear morning. Had the worst road a part of the day we have had since we
crossed the summit. Made 15 miles Camped near a small branch. Sage & water
plenty Grass poor Saw George Perkins He Is camped about 4 miles east of us with
some of his train He got some of his oxen lamed yesterday Wells Is some miles
west of us Cortez kept his bed all day

S.16th Cloudy nearly all day Made 20 miles Camped a few miles east of Warm
Springs Rough roads Several of our wagon wheels are getting very frail Cortez'
complaint is in his left hand and arm. Docters say It is scurvy. Not any better

108

Fuel & grass good No water for the stock

S.17th Cloudy at sunrise Thunder and black clouds but no rain Made 19 miles Camped near a small branch Grass and sage good Water poor. Roads good

M.18th. Cloudy at sunrise Nearly all day. Made 20 miles. Camped in the Thousand Springs Valey So we did last night We passed some warm springs, or rather a branch of warm water. Had good roads

T.19th Clear and cool morning Made 15 miles Camped on Canon Creek Fuel and water plenty, grass poor Cortez still keeps his wagon. Perkins at our camp Some of his train before and some behind We are now on the waters of Humbolt

W 20th Rained a few drops at sunrise Clear from 7 a.m. Made 18 miles Camped Sage and water 1/4 mile from the camp. Grass midleng John Walker and McCamman sick Cortez menting slow if any We lost a fine work ox by alkily

Th 21st Fine clear morning Crossed on a bridge a branch of Humboldt and also two other branches of the same stream Both bad crossings Before noon made 14 miles Camped near the river Travelled none in the afternoon. Grass water & fuel good Small shower of rain after dark

F.22nd Clear morning. No rain to lay the dust. Fruit lost one of his work oxen Made 19 miles Camped near the west branch of Humboldt River Grass good Fuel and water 1/2 mile from camp Cortez not getting better

S.23rd Clear and pleasent morning Made 18 miles Camped on the river Grass sage and water good Three of Walkers and one of our men sick Cortez no better Weather warm

S.24th Clear morning. Cortez some better. So is our sick man Made 10 miles Camped close to the river Sage & grass midling. We stoped early as the road now leaves the river over some steep hills for 12 or 15 miles without water and not much grass if any This is the first day that we saw no snow since the 5th of June

M 25th Clear morning Made 17 miles Camped near Blue Creek Grass fuel & water good. One of our mares(nancy) died The dust in the afternoon was realy disagreeable particularly for those in the rear of the train

T.26th Clear morning Enoch Walker lost the tire of one of the family wagons wheels Found one nearly where he missed his that answered the purpose which was put on. Made 17 miles over rough and stony road Camped in a ravine Sage plenty Water for stock and cooking and grass scarse

W 27th Clear and warm day We nooned near the river There is a beautiful spring which afords a great quantity of good and cool water All the men on duty except Cortez He keeps his bed all the time Made 19 miles Camped on the river Sage scarse Grass midling Franklin yesterday sold one of the work oxen and a yearling heiffer Both unfit to travel There are a number of persons camped near the road ready to buy all the lame and given out cattle at a low prise say from $5. to $20 a head Franklin got but $15 for both of his This ox had been not in a thriving condition since we crossed the Missourie River

Th 28th Clear day. Made 14 miles Camped on Rippel Creek. Sage and water poor. Grass midling Franklin took sick last evening. Not on duty the day. Cortez mending very slow. Walkers lost a fine bull last night. It is supposed he took into the river Could not reach the shore and drowend

F.29th Clear morning A contravacy took place just at the point of leaving the camp between Fruit and one of his men(Griffith Johns) Fruit having no weapon, Johns having a revolver and a large knife In the fray Fruit got the knife. Johns discharged two loads out of his revolver One took effect of Fruit The ball entered his groins and lodged somewhere. John Walker starded for a docter He is not returned The danger of the wound not ascertained The pain however is great. Johns made his escape, although several of the men were in search of him It is now nearly sunset No docter as yet We remained in camp the day. Poor water for

110

men and beasts

S. 30th No docter to examine Fruits wound at 7 o clock a.m. He rested bad the later part of the night Franklin some better Cortez mending some. Some of Walkers men went in search of a docter at 3 o clock a.m. That was the time John Walker returned being disappointed after hard days travel. We got a docter about 10 o clock a.m. he examined the wound The ball was not extracted. Gave and left medecine Talked flattering We moved 8 miles Camped Water sage and grass good.

s.31st. Clear morning Fruit died near sunrise About 12M we enterred Fruit without a coffin of any kind Made a vault in the grave and with some boards and willows We covered his body over and filled up the grave and covered the whole with stone His grave is about 8 miles wist of Ripple Creek on the left side of the road on rocky and high knole with a head board containing his name age and when he died and the name of his last residence It was a solomn and heart renting case

AUGUST 1st.M. Clear morning made 18 miles Camped near a small branch Sage, water and grass poor A part of the road was very rough and stoney Wagon wheels given way Dust encreasing

T.2d Clear morning Made 14 miles Camped Water fuel & grass scarse Franklin still on the sick list Cortez mending if any slowly. John Walker gone forward yesterday intended to be in advance of the train upwards of one hundred miles in a few days His object is to arrest Griffith.

W.3rd Clear and warm day. The forenoon heavy sand. Made 15 miles. Camped close by the river. Grass midling Sage scarse. Franklin not much better I am nearly run down

Th 4th Clear & warm day Made 15 miles Camped not far from the river Grass fuel & water poor Franklin mending some Rough roads & heavy sand. Saw snow not a great distance from the road

F.5th Beautiful morning Made 18 miles Camped near the river. Grass water & fuel midling. Forded Rush Creek Good ford Rather deep Some of the wagons took in considerable water saw snow. One of our cows died

S 6th Clear day Heavy sandy roads Made 18 miles Camped near to the river Water plenty Grass & fuel scarse We passed upwards of 20 dead oxen and cows Franklin's case is scurfy Cortez mending slowly

S.7th. Clear morning. Stock this morning unrully wanting grass Made 20 miles Camped near the river. Grass poor. John Walker came to the camp Heard not anythink of Griffith Both the boys not any better

M.8th. Clear morning Made 14 miles Camped on the bank of the river. Grass fair. Franklin no better, Cortez mending. The men are gathering grass for the desert

T.9th Clear morning I feel uncomfortable on account of my old complaint with discharging my water which has not troubled me since we were on the journey. Cortez bought a light wagon at $5 Sold two cows at $10 The both were on the point of failing to travel

W.10th Clear day I am not much better Made 16 miles Camped at a spring Rough roads

SEPTEMBER 25th Since the 10 ultt I have been on the sick list unable to continue my journal daily. Sufice it to say that the whole train got at the settlement in Rogue River Valy on the 3rd day of September 1853 All in good health except myself and Cortez and Franklin who ware still cripled in their arms with the scurffe. Isaac Hill was the second house we came too there We found wells in camp Asa Fordys about 12 miles lower down in the value. He had been attackted by the Indians a few days before we arived Was wounded with two leaden balls and one arrow None proved dangerous Hugh Smith killed and one of his other men wounded. As respects the road it was rougher and hillier then any we came over before. We had to travel one whole day and night in crossing the desert without water or grass for men and of stock Made during that time about 40 miles. We during that time lost one work ox. In the whole our animals that we got into The valey look well considering the long journey they had to perform since then the boys and Walkers were imployed in making a location for themselves. The boys have made their locations for themselves and for me about 12 miles east of Jacksonville Jackson County all in one track The Walkers have made their location about 10 miles west of us in the same valey in one body We all have had some difficulties in making our locations on account of so many land claimers that do not intend to make it their homes Some of our and Walkers land located is claimed by some of those gentries. Wells purchased his location, and so did Fordyce. Wells about 4 miles east and so is Fordyce Walkers men have left them after their arival in the valey in a few days Some of our done the same All seeking to make their fortune Some of our men still with us at work for the boys This is to be the end of this journal

SEPTEMBER 27th The boys made a location of a section and one have of land all in one body We all camped on it from the 12th to the 15th instant. Franklin first Cortez second and we the last We have now 2 cabins Raised logs on the ground for the third Bords nearly made to cover them

OCTOBER 4th This day mother & my two youngest daughters and myself moved our beds into the cabin build by my two sons for us with the intention to sleep under a roof which none of us did since the 23d day of March last The cabin is build of round logs 14 by 16 feet Stone chimey. Floor laid with good slabs from the mill No door or class Window cloth is to be the substitute

A NOVEL

FRUIT

THE STORY OF THE MYER AND WALKER FAMILIES WAGON TREK TO OREGON

By
Ken And Laura Jones

Figure 42   Nathaniel & Mary Myer
Mary holding baby Frances

MARCH 21,1853

Nathaniel Myer hit the alarm button on the bedstand clock, almost before the alarm sounded. "Mary", gently caressing his wife, "Are you awake?"

"Nathan, I've hardly slept any, thinking about what's going to happen to us!

"Now, Mary, don't you fret", his comforting voice responded, as his bare feet touched the cold floor, on this frigid Iowa March morning. "I'll get the stove fired up, and put on some water, while you get dressed." On his way to the kitchen, Nathaniel lit a couple of lamps to relieve that extra worry that comes from the dark side of dawn.

Nathaniel, at age 66, and Mary, age 61, would be spending the next five or six months traveling by wagon train on their journey to Oregon! Their wagon was packed with what little of their forty years of life together, that would fit in that wagon box, 12 feet long and 3 1/2 feet wide.

Over a bowl of hot oatmeal, and a cup of steaming coffee, the two talked of their future.

"We've talked about this a lot, Mary. All of our kids and grandkids are going to Oregon, and we don't want to be left behind! Besides, if we didn't sell the house, and use our savings, the kids wouldn't be able to go."

"I know you are right, Nathan, but we are comfortable here, and besides, we are old. You've got peeing problems, and only one eye. I've got the rheumatiz in my fingers and knees. I'm just plain scared!"

"You know Mamma, so am I, but we are going to let the Lord know that, with His help and guidance, we are going to make it to Oregon, safe and sound!"

Nathaniel hitched the two black mares to their wagon, as Mary gathered up the last of her personal possessions. With one last look at what was left of their past, they headed down the road to an uncertain future.

116

Late afternoon found Nathaniel and Mary arriving at the farm of their son, Franklin. Their other son, Cortez, and his family had spent last night here, helping to get all the livestock, tack, and provisions ready for the long journey ahead. The elder Myer's three daughters, and grandchildren were also here. Discussion around the dinner table that evening, centered on many questions concerning the trip.

"How many head of cattle are you taking along?" Nathaniel asked his two sons.

"With the cattle, Franklin bought yesterday, plus what I have, we should have close to eighty head.", Cortez replied.

"We also have five teams of oxen, and two horse teams", Franklin added.

"How on earth are we going to get all of that to Oregon, without getting lost!", Franklin's wife, Dolly, queried.

"That should be no problem", her husband responded. "We have seven hired hands, in addition to us."

"We also have a copy of Horn's guide book, which describes the trail all the way to Oregon," Nathaniel added. "I'll be using it for a reference, to locate where we are, in my diary. Besides, we'll be catching up with the Walker train, and that will give us a lot more hands."

"Elizabeth," her concerned mother-in-law inquired, "What about baby Frances? Can you take care of a four month old baby, in a crowded little wagon, for the time it takes to get to Oregon?"

"I'll manage. She is a strong baby, and easy to take care of. I'll play with her a lot, along the way, and with my quilting work, the days will go by quickly."

Questions continued to flow, until, finally, someone said it was time to go to bed. Tomorrow will be the last day to get ready.

W. C. Myer   Elizabeth Myer

Figures 43-46

B. F. Myer   Dolly Myer

MARCH 22, 1853

This, the final day of preparations, found the Myer family frantically
engaged in last minute chores. Freezing weather did not deter the men, as they
made necessary adjustments to the wagons and teams. They had few problems with
the horse teams, but the oxen were a different story. Franklin commented to his
brother, "I understand that oxen make better teams for a long trip like this,
but our tack doesn't fit, and we don't have any experience trying to drive
them."

"Well, Frank, we need to adjust these harnesses, and then we'll try them
out. By tomorrow we should be practiced enough to get by; besides, some of our
hired men have driven ox teams without any problems." "Yeah, I guess you are
right," Frank responded. "I'm going to get dad to come out here to help us. He
has worked ox teams, farming."

Meanwhile, the women were busy, preparing as much food as possible for the
long trip. Bacon, and ham had been cured. Most any other meat would spoil.
Franklin's wife, Dolly, had made some dried venison jerky that would be good for
snacks along the trail. Containers of flour, coffee, lard, beans, dried fruit,
and sugar were already packed in the wagons, as were pots and pans, along with
dishware. By mid afternoon, everything seemed to be ready.

"Let's sit down and rest a bit, before fixing dinner," Elizabeth suggested,
as she picked up her quilting project.

"Do you think you will have time for quilting on the trail, what with the
baby and all?" her sister, Temperance asked.

"Oh dear, I just can't imagine what will happen. I get so worried that I
pick up my quilting, to get my mind on something else! I know the rest of you

are exited about going, and I try to be; but—"

"Elizabeth, we all have these fears of doubt and uncertainty," her mother-in-law reassured. "That is going to be such a beautiful quilt, with those bright red and green colors. You just quilt when you feel the need, and we will all help you with little Frances."

Prayers of a safe jouney, were whispered at the evening meal, as their last dinner at home was served.

The Walkers, and their crew, having left several days ago, were camped along the Des Moines river, about one hundred miles west of their home in Farmington. The group left early to make arrangements for a ferry crossing, and to search out suitable grass for the livestock. They were to await here for the Myer train. The Walker train consisted of three brothers, Enoch, John, and Fruit, their wives, and children, and several hired men. John was not married. They too, had a good sized herd of livestock.

That evening the group huddled around a campfire, warding off the chill of the Iowa, early spring. Griffith Johns, one of the hired hands, mouthed soulful tunes, on his harmonica, the folk music of mistreated slaves. Mary Ann, a daughter of Nathaniel and Mary, arranged a blanket over her slender, young body, and snuggled into the warm awaiting arms of her husband. The stars were out, creating within her, an excitement for the future.

MARCH 23, 1853

"Hallelujah!" exclaimed Cortez, leading the assortment of wagons, oxen, horses, and cattle, as the Myer train began the march to Oregon. All told, there were seven wagons, twenty oxen, eight horses, seventy-three head of cattle, seven hired hands, and eighteen members of the Myer family.

This was not to be a long day of travel, but rather one of adjusting, experimenting, and generally getting used to the requirements of this mode of transportation. Thankfully, the teams behaved well, and no major problems occurred. By noon, the train arrived at the Fordyce farm, where they had arranged to camp for the night. The Fordyce's greeted them all, with a lunch of beef stew, and freshly baked bread.

"Now don't you even think about fixing us dinner, or breakfast," Dolly directed Mrs. Fordyce. "we need to learn how to set up camp, and fix for ourselves."

Everyone had chores to do the rest of the day. The livestock needed water and grass; tents were set up for sleeping; the children gathered wood, and filled buckets of water for cooking and washing; the women were busy preparing for the evening meal, and making beds in the tents and wagons. They were all getting into the spirit of pioneer life.

Evening found the Myer family enjoying a campfire, the first of many to come, on their long journey west. Elizabeth, after tucking her baby into her cradle, picked up her quilting. While adding another patch or two, she softly sang little Frances to sleep.

"Sleeping in these cramped quarters is going to be a challenge," Mary lamented to Nathaniel, as she spread the blankets on the floor of the wagon.

"Mary, my dear loving spouse, this closeness is only good for newlyweds, and oldtimers, needing the intimacy that this bed offers. I shall be delighted to share it with you! "

"Well, Nathan, if you put it that way, will you fetch us a pan of hot water from the fire? After a day in the dust of the trail, we need to freshen up a bit! "

March 31, 1853

After leaving their camp at the Fordyces, the Myer train treked slowly northwesterly into the center of Iowa. They were following the Des Moines river, headed for the Walker camp, which they would reach tonight.

Few problems had occurred to date. Well, not really a problem, but Mary and Nathaniel slept in a tent the second night out. Jackson, one of the hired hands, came down with the mumps! Nathaniel offered to drive his wagon. A mishap occurred; Smith, another hired hand, was kicked by one of the horses. While very sore, he was able to remain on duty.

The weather had been typically March, with wind, rain, snow, and freezing temperatures. At times the wagons stalled in muddy ruts, and blizzard conditions. If it wasn't mud, it was dust!

One of the oxen "took sick", and was left to die. A young heifer "dropped" a still born calf. Another wandered off during the evening, causing Franklin to lose most of a night's sleep. A second oxen "took sick", but kept up with train, while a third one became lame.

These were normal days in the life of the pioneers!

Shouts of welcome rang out from the Walkers, as the Myer train came into view. After lunch, Fruit and John Walker brought the Myers up to date. "Enoch has gone ahead to make arrangements for ferrying us across the Des Moines river, and then on to Council Bluffs, to see about crossing the Missouri," Fruit informed the group. "We are to remain here, until he returns, or receive word from him to meet up with him at the crossing."

For several days, the Walkers, and Myers remained camped along the Des Moines river, waiting for word from Enoch. Keeping the livestock in good grass was a problem. An attempt was made to build a large corral, but heavy winds defeated the project.

The idle days of no travel allowed the members of the two trains to become good friends, and a working team, to help in overcoming problems encountered in the days and months ahead.

APRIL 8, 1853

Enoch Walker returned to the camp the evening of April 5th. Heavy rains had swollen the Des Moines river, delaying a ferry crossing for several days. Wagon trains were backed up at the river, awaiting its recession.

By the 7th of April, the weather had improved into a sunny, spring-like day. The two families decided to move camp five miles up the river, to find better feed for the livestock. Not finding sufficient pasture land, Cortez and Fruit took two wagons to a village nearby, where they were able to purchase supplemental feed. Keeping all of their animals properly fed was becoming a major problem!

The warm day created a good opportunity for the rest of the group, to wash clothes and bathe, in a slough of the river. Little Frances seemed to enjoy the chilly water, as her mother gently submerged her tiny feet. The rest of the women frolicked in a shallow eddy, secluded from view. Griffith Johns decided to try his luck, fishing along the bank. Before long, he had caught a mess of trout sufficient to give the entire camp a tasty tidbit for dinner! As he was cleaning the catch, he was embarrassed to find the bathing women within his view. Quickly, he retreated without being detected! Since he was a hired hand, that could have been disasterous. None the less, he did find the incident rather stimulating.

Unbeknownst to Johns, Franklin's daughter, Judith, had witnessed the scene, and feeling that it was a deliberate act, reported it to her father. "Papa, I saw Mr. Johns peeking through the bushes, at Mother, and the other ladies, when they were down at the river!"

After giving the matter some thought, Franklin decided to talk to Fruit about it, for Johns was under his employment. A short-tempered man, Fruit was

125

furious, when Franklin divulged this to him.

"Griffith, you have some explaining to do, spying on our women, when they were bathing in the river!" Fruit charged.

"Now wait a minute, Fruit, that is not the way it happened!"

Fruit, reluctantly accepted Johns' account, although, in the back of his mind, he still had a doubt. The matter was dropped, and Fruit relayed this to his brother-in-law.

In spite of the confrontation, everyone enjoyed the pan-fried trout, that was Griffith Johns' treat. After dinner, he further redeemed himself, by entertaining the group with his harmonica. Nathaniel, an old fiddler, added to the evening festivities, as he played his lively tunes, to the delight of his audience. Mary commented to Fruit, as they were crawling into bed.

"Honey, wasn't that a wonderful trout dinner? Mr. Johns is such a nice man, and I really love his harmonica playing! ''

APRIL 14, 1853

Two of the Walker brothers, Enoch and Fruit, conversed about the weather halting their crossing of the River. Fruit offered, "If we don't get moving pretty quick, I think we may lose the good attitude we have maintained so far."

"Yeah, you are right about that, Fruit. We need to move the livestock to better grazing."

"Maybe we should move our camp closer to the crossing. What do you think, Enoch?"

"Why don't you and I take a ride over to the Ferry Crossing. We can look for better grass along the way." After informing the group of their intention, Cortez replied, "I would like to join you, but we are going to brand some stock today, and Smith is too sick to work. Our cattle got out last night, looking for feed. I sure hope you find some better grazing!" After traveling two miles or so, the two men reached the ferry crossing. The river had receded, somewhat, and with another couple of days of fair weather, they should be able to safely cross.

"The livestock aren't going to feed any better around here," Enoch commented.

"Why don't we see if we can camp on that farm over yonder. They might have some feed we can buy," Fruit responded.

With arrangements made for their arrival in a couple of days, the brothers headed back to their camp.

Meanwhile, Griffith Johns succeeded in catching another mess of trout sufficient for the evening meal.

"Would you like me to help you clean the fish?", Sarah, Nathaniel's seventeen year old daughter, asked of Griffith.

"I would be delighted, ma'am," Griffith responded, handing her an extra knife, along with a string of fish. "Do you know how to clean trout, Sarah?"

"I have watched my father do it."

Sarah's sister, Mary, observing the conversation, felt annoyed at herself for wanting to intercede.

"Fruit won't clean his fish, so I have lots of experience," Mary quipped. "Let me do it, Sarah."

"No, you are always putting me down like this. I want to learn how to do it!" Sarah complained.

Amused at the sisters' rivalry, Griffith offered, "I'll get another knife, and we can all do it."

Noticing that her husband had returned, Mary apologized for interfering, and hurried to greet Fruit.

APRIL 18, 1853

Moderate rain continued for the next couple of days, forcing the group to remain at their camp. Enough feed was purchased from neighboring farms to maintain the livestock, but the lack of grass, along with the inactivity of the group, began to wear. Finally, on the 17th, after a frosty morning, the warm sun greeted them, allowing the two trains to move on to the Des Moines river crossing.

"We managed to ferry some horse wagons across today", one of the Ferrymen advised Enoch Walker. "If the weather holds, we should be able to get your wagons across tomorrow."

The evening was spent making preparations for the river crossing. High water required that the wagons be calked to prevent water from getting inside them. Bedding and clothing were removed from the floor. Repairs were made to the yokes, and wagon wheels. The fair weather, and the expectations of tomorrow's crossing had improved the morale of everyone. Mary Walker found Griffith Johns calking the seams of her wagon.

"I'll be putting up a tent for you and Fruit to sleep in tonight, to give this wax a chance to dry," Griffith commented. "Let me help you. Fruit is out with the cattle, but I have helped him put up tents lots of times."

The two worked well together, and, in no time, the tent was erected. Mary secured the bedding and clothing from the wagon, and as they were making the bed in the tent, Griffith, joked "I could surely enjoy sleeping under those covers!"

Not knowing quite what he meant by that, Mary circumvented the statement by replying," Where will you be sleeping tonight?"

"There is still a lot of calking left for me to do, and I'll be spelling Fruit, tending the cattle, later on. Maybe I can catch a few winks in between"

"Well, I will be thinking of you out there in the chill of the night, while I am resting in my nice, warm bed!" They both laughed, as Griffith returned to his calking.

"Keep those teams moving!" the ferryman yelled at the drivers, as they forded the river. The day was threatened by dark thunder clouds, but so far, no rain. Nathaniel, driving the lead wagon, made it safely across. At one point in the river, the wagon floated, but the horses kept their footing.

"Watch that deep hole, Cortez. Keep the horses moving, or you will be swamped by the current!" Nathaniel yelled to his son.

By noon, the trains were safely across, and on their way west towards the great Missouri.

APRIL 22, 1853

The miserable part of the emigration began to emerge. Muddy roads, through treacherous sloughs, blustery weather, starving cattle, sickness, and a host of other problems took their toll.

"How are things going with the wagons, Dad?" Cortez asked, as he rode up to his father, from the rear of the train, where he had been driving the cattle.

"Not so good, son. These sloughs are bogging us down. One of the wagons got swamped. We had to add another team to get them out. One of my mares lost a shoe in the mud, and an ox yoke on your wagon broke. Enoch's wagon team got scared, and ran a distance. Mrs. Walker finally got them stopped, but she and her daughter, Martha are still crying from being so frightened!"

"Well, we're having problems too. I'm afraid we are going to lose some of the calves. We just don't have enough feed, and these muddy sloughs are wearing them out. Some of our men are feeling poorly. Thrash is sick in one of the wagons, and not able to work. Temperance and Elizabeth are back there, helping us."

The disagreeable weather continued, with thunder storms, and high winds, as the wagon trains slowly treked westward over the next few days. The night of the 22nd found the group entrenched in their tents and wagons, trying to escape the fierce storm.

"Nathaniel, the rain is blowing in the wagon, and soaking our bedding," Mary complained, as they tried to keep warm under the blankets. Sleep was impossible, as they huddled together, trying to stay warm.

"There is nothing we can do now, Mary. Just stay in my arms, and we will be OK until morning"

"Papa, our tent blew down, and we are soaking wet," Sarah cried, as she and

Temperance scrambled into the wagon.

Other tents suffered the same fate. The women and children were racing around, looking for shelter. Some of them tried to build a fire, without success. The men were out trying to contain the frightened livestock.

"Griffith, you'd better go back to the wagons," Fruit requested. "They are going to need all the help they can get, to weather this storm!"

Griffith found the camp in complete disarray. All of the wagons were soaked, and only two tents remained upright. Opening the flap of one, he found Mary Walker frightened, but dry.

"Oh Fruit, I am so glad you are back!" she whispered, as she pulled Griffith out of the storm, and into the tent. Before he could say anything, Griffith felt Mary's trembling body next to his. "Griffith, is that you? I thought you were Fruit," her startled voice cried out.

"I'm sorry that I startled you, Mary. Fruit asked me to help you cope with this storm. Your tent, and one other is all that is left standing. I came to ask that you share your tent with some of the others that are huddled in the rain."

"Of course I will," Mary quickly responded. I apologize for my childish actions, but all that thunder and lightning, and the wind blowing, really had me terrified. Thank you for coming!" Griffith soon had everyone under cover, and out of the storm.

APRIL 23, 1853

Morning arrived, with the disheveled campers continuing to
suffer from the relentless storm. Torrents of rain, mixed with hail, stung their
faces. Starting a fire was futile; clothing and bedding was soaked. Breakfast
was limited to soggy bread and dried fruit. The cattle could be heard mournfully
mooing from the lack of feed. There was none to be had.

"We are in bad shape, and need to get out of here," Enoch complained. "If we
don't get some feed for the livestock soon, we will lose them for sure! I'll
take some wagons and men on ahead to look for some. The rest of you come on as
soon as you can."

By 8:00 a.m., shortly after Enoch's departure, the rest of the group trudged
out of camp, facing a muddy road, and a blustery day. Worried about the cattle,
and short-handed, Fruit decided to stay with the herd.

"Griffith, I need you to drive the wagon today, while I tend to these poor
animals. With all this rain and mud, I don't think Mary can handle the team."

"You go ahead and drive the wagon, Fruit, and I'll take care of the herd,"
Griffith offered.

"No, i'm too worried about some of our calves. I wouldn't be able to keep my
mind on driving the wagon, thinking about them."

When Griffith caught up with the wagons, he found Mary, huddled in a wet
blanket, barely in control of her wagon team.

"Fruit asked me to give you a hand, Mary, while he takes care of the herd.
I'll tie my horse to the wagon, and take over the driving." As Griffith climbed
up beside Mary, he suggested,

"Why don't you crawl back in the wagon, and try to warm up?"

"Well, I can't get warmed up, wearing these wet clothes. Perhaps I can find something dry to put on," she responded, as she rummaged through her things. Mary's cold, soft fingers ached, as she attempted to unbutton the back of her wet, clinging dress.

"Griffith, I just can't get these buttons loose, at the back of my dress.

"Turn your back to me, and I'll do it for you. Don't worry, I'll keep my eyes closed," he assured Mary, noticing her hesitant look. Griffith kept his word, but could not help his excitement, as his fingers touched her smooth soft skin, while he groped for the buttons down her slender back.

Griffith coaxed the team into motion, as Mary put on dry clothing. Returning to sit by him, she laughed "Griffith, your fingers were cold!"

"Well, I haven't had much experience undressing a pretty woman, with my eyes closed," Griffith replied, trying to sound debonair.

"You haven't made love to a woman before?"

"That's like me asking if you have had a man other than Fruit!"

The storm continued as the wagons reached the crossing of the Middle River. Mary and Nathaniel, along with the children, remained in the wagon, as the rest braved the weather to set up camp. In spite of the wind and rain, a fire was started, and a canvas was spread over tall poles, above it. Rope was strung in an attempt to dry the wet clothing and bedding.

Enoch and his crew returned with their wagons full of corn for the stock. Fruit greeted his brother, with much concern.

"Three of the calves are dead, and I don't think another one is going to make it. Thank God you found some corn!

"I never should have done this to you, Mary," Nathaniel lamented to his shivering wife, as he held her wet body next to his. "I know, with this terrible weather, your rheumatiz must be really bad!"

"Now Nathan," trying to comfort her husband, "Once this storm is over, we will all feel a lot better." Mary knew, as well as Nathan, at their advanced years, their chilled, weakened bodies were threatened with pneumonia, or even worse, the dreaded cholera that had taken so many emigrants along this trail. She also felt that their determination, and with God's blessing, they would survive! Mary heard Elizabeth softly crying, as she held little Frances to her breast. "There's no need for crying, Liz! This storm will pass, and we will be just fine. When you're through feeding Frances, I will change her, while you get warm by that nice fire. I see Cortez huddled by it, drinking a cup of coffee. You go join him, and you'll feel better."

"Thank you, mother Mary. If you don't mind, I'll just do that. Forgive me for these falling tears, but I am so weary, and my wet clothes chill my body until I can hardly move. What will become of us! I am so afraid for my baby!" Elizabeth sobbed, as she handed her to Mary.

"She is a good, strong little girl, Liz. With all the love and attention she gets, Frances is bound to be healthy and happy." As her fingers gently touched the baby's smiling face, Mary silently prayed for her family's safety.

APRIL 26, 1853

The rain continued to punish the camp for another night and day, until, at sunrise on the 25th, they awoke, shivering, to a frosty, but sunny morning!

Warm sunshine created a steamy campsite, as bedding, clothing, and mother nature began to dry out from those stormy days. The cattle crossed the stream the day before, to feed on better grass, as Enoch's supply of corn had been consumed, with no more to be found at any price. Another strategy session was necessary, as the river was too high to ford.

"Let's spend the day camped right here, to let everything get dry," Cortez suggested. "Maybe by tomorrow, the river will be low enough to cross." The Middle River, under normal conditions, was not deemed difficult to ford.

As the day progressed, a rather large Wagon train arrived at the crossing. Impatient to move on, they began falling large cottonwood trees along the river bank. They were placed across the stream, in a manner that allowed the wagon axels to slide on the logs, pulled by oxen on the other side. Most of their wagons were bridged across by nightfall. The rest would cross tomorrow.

Watching the remaining wagons cross the following morning, Fruit and Cortez approached their wagonmaster.

"That is quite an ingenious way you bridged that stream," Fruit complimented the wagonmaster.

"We could use those logs to get our wagons across," Cortez added.

"We plan to buck up the logs for firewood, since fuel is pretty scarce along this trail," the wagonmaster countered. "Our schedule won't allow us to wait for all your wagons to cross."

At this point in the conversation, Franklin Myer joined the group. He had been scouting around for corn for the livestock.

"I arranged to buy a cord of firewood for $5.00 from a farmer on up the road. How about if we pay you $5.00 for the bridge, and you can buy wood already cut and cured? That will save all of us some time." That, being satisfactory with the Wagonmaster, solved their river crossing dilemma.

After the bridge crossing with the wagons, another train arrived.

"That bridge cost us $5.00, and we'll sell it to you for the same amount," Fruit offered to their group.

"You can't stop us from using those logs. They are on a public stream, and we intend to use them, without paying you extortion!" their spokesman threatened.

"Quick-tempered Fruit retorted in anger, "We intend to remove those logs, and use them for firewood!" With that, he yelled to his crew, "Hitch those oxen to the logs, and drag them across." As the men began to comply, a scuffle, between the two, was thwarted by the rest of the group.

"Here is your $5.00," offered one of others, as he handed Fruit the money. Fortunately, a dangerous confrontation was avoided.

The next day the Myer/Walker trains gained only three miles, as they camped in a forest, looking for the cattle. The herd had been brought here yesterday, for better grazing.

With better weather, the families were back in good spirits. The women and children wandered through the forest, picking wild flowers and mushrooms, while the men searched for cattle. Elizabeth found time to work on her quilt, which she had neglected during those stormy days. Her young sister, Sarah, helped with watching over Frances, who suddenly found mobility, as she was learning to crawl.

"Liz, do you have any extra sewing material?" Sarah inquired. Frances needs something to protect her tender legs when she crawls around on this rough ground. I can't keep her on her blanket anymore! Maybe I could make her a little play suit."

Yesterday, after the wagons crossed, Griffith Johns took advantage of the river by catching another mess of fish. With the morels that were picked today, a feast of fried trout, smothered with delicious mushrooms was prepared for dinner.

Refreshed from two warms days, with little travel, the trains again headed west. Unfortunately, the heavy rains had swollen the sloughs, making passage a challenge. High water leaked into the wagons, and they were plagued again with wet blankets and clothes. Fruit Walker's team floundered in one slough, with the horses unable to pull out their heavy hooves buried in the muddy bottom. The wagon was unhitched, and with another team of horses, the swamped team was rescued. In another bog, the tongue straps on Enoch's wagon gave way, as the team attempted to struggle through. Repairs were tedious, for the men were required to work in the cold, brackish swamp, the habitat of snakes, and leeches. In spite of these problems, the wagons were eighteen miles further west, toward Oregon, when they camped for the night.

Much of the next day was spent repairing the wagons and tack. Some of the Walker's horses had wandered off during the night, requiring John Walker, Fruit's brother, to search for them. Fruit had left yesterday for Council Bluffs. With a late start, and two more sloughs, the group still traveled eight miles by sundown. John Walker arrived with the horses a short time later.

In Fruit's absence, Griffith helped Mary erect her sleeping tent. They had become good friends, enjoying their moments together.

"Are you managing OK, without Fruit?" Griffith questioned Mary.

"Well, these nights are chilly, and I miss his warm body beside me; but I am doing tolerably well."

"Mary, I wish I could take his place," Griffith laughed. "I will pitch my tent close by though; just in case you need me."

Mary sat upright in her bed, awakened by the awesome flash of lightning, followed by the threatening rumbling of thunder! Gusts of wind ripped through her precarious tent. "Why isn't Fruit here to hold and protect me from this awful storm," she cried to herself. "I am so afraid!" At the next gust, Mary was entangled in bedding and canvas, as the tent collapsed around her. Griffith pulled her from the debris, as she sobbed, hysterically, in his arms.

"Don't be frightened, Mary," Griffith pleaded, as his lips caressed her forehead. "It's just a passing thunderstorm that will be over soon," trying to calm her.

"Please don't leave me here alone. Griffith. I'm just so terrified by this dreadful, black, stormy night!"

MAY 3, 1853

Nathaniel mentioned the storm in his May 1st diary entry:

"Wind blowed hard last night and this morning. Tent blowed down in the night. Tremendous rain storm at 7 o'clock a.m."

The next few days, though trying, were rather uneventful. Several streams were crossed, with some requiring wagon repairs. Feed for the cattle continued to be a problem, but they were in reasonably good condition. Fruit returned from Council Bluffs, having made arrangements for crossing the Missouri River. Their wagon trains would arrive there in a few days. "I'm so glad you are back, safe," Mary greeted her husband, as she rushed into his arms. "I have had a miserable time while you were gone. If it weren't for Mr. Johns, I don't know what I would have done!" relating to Fruit, her frightening night of the storm. The wagons passed by a large farm, at which, Franklin negotiated the purchase of eight bushels of badly needed corn for the horses. As they proceeded west, the rivers became narrow and deep, with high banks. Fording these would be hazardous, if not impossible. Fortunately, earlier emigrants built bridges for crossing the most difficult streams. For the most part, the days were sunny and warm. Spring was evident, as they passed a plum orchard in full bloom. Honey bees were busily engaged in pollination, buzzing by the hundreds, from blossom to blossom. Spring time in Iowa can create nostalgic visions of picnics and wildflowers, the song of the meadowlark, and the fresh, green leaves, renewing the branches of deciduous trees. The trade off is dust! Wagons and cattle created a trail of choking dust that stifled the enthusiasm of any traveler caught in its path!

Camped for the night, along a wooded creek, the families were startled by the arrival of a dozen or so Indians. Cortez and Fruit came forward to greet them.

"Our provisions are too meagre to offer you food or drink, but you are welcome to the warmth of our fire," Cortez offered.

"We accept your friendship, with ours in return," their leader responded, as he dismounted from his colorful spotted pony. The Indians gathered aound the fire, while the women and children scurried to the protection of their wagons.

"My brothers are in need of food, or money in which to buy food and clothing for their families. I am Shenandoah, Chief of the Nishnabotna. You are welcome in our territory.

"You are very kind, Chief Shenandoah," Fruit replied. "We too are in need. Our livestock are in need of corn, and one of our team horses is lame. We have little money to cover our long journey to Oregon. We would be honored to exchange what little extra we have, for these much needed things." Shenandoah gazed into Fruit's unflinching eyes, and then at the gentle smiling face of Cortez. After what seemed like minutes of silence, Shenandoah spoke, "You speak with wise words for protection of your brothers, as have I. Your offer is fair." The Indians mounted their horses, and disappeared into the night.

MAY 6, 1853

During breakfast the next morning, Chief Shenandoah reappeared, bringing his eldest son with him. Fruit greeted the two, inviting them to share the camp breakfast.

"You have brought corn for our livestock, for which we are very grateful." Fruit acknowledged, noticing the loaded cart. "we return your kindness with what little we can spare, to help feed your family, and your people."

After breakfast the exchange was completed. The tension gripping the camp, began to ease, when the Chief and his son disappeared from view.

Fifteen miles closer to the Missouri, the families camped at the Silver Creek crossing. With luck, they would reach the great river tomorrow. The wagons had crossed several bridged streams on the way. One, a toll bridge, was well constructed while the others were not. They were learning, from experience, a lot about bridges. At Silver Creek, the bridge had been destroyed, apparently from high water. Leaning on their past experience, the men proceeded to rebuild it. Upon completion, the livestock crossed for better grass on the opposite side.

Excitement, along with anxiety, mounted as the wagons crossed the bridge the following morning, their day's destination being the Missouri River. Not only was this the largest stream they would cross, but, on the other side, they would find unsettled wilderness.

The eighteen mile trip, compared to past days, was relatively routine. A party of ten Indians passed by them, without incident.
Sections of the road were rough and rocky, causing a wagon wheel to break. Temporary repairs were made. The cattle had little grass in which to graze along the way.

Late that afternoon, they reached the Missouri. After finding a suitable campsite along the river bottom, Fruit and Cortez left to arrange for their ferry crossing in the morning. They found the river had receded from the level it was when Fruit checked it several days earlier. The ferrymen indicated there should not be a problem in crossing.

The evening air was inviting, with a universe of sparkling stars spreading from all directions. After dinner, the group lingered around the campfire, conversing about tomorrow, and the days of uncertainty to follow. John Walker, having studied a little astronomy, pointed out some stars and constellations.

"If you find yourself lost at night, the stars can help you," John explained, as he located the North Star, Polaris. Griffith Johns accepted requests of folk songs, playing his harmonica until the campers reluctantly retired for the night.

MAY 9, 1853

The big concern about crossing the Missouri River was almost anti–climatic. The water level was ideal for the cattle to swim, and the ferrymen handled the wagons without incident. The unexpected difficulty surfaced with the crossing of a slough, some three miles west. Wagons that weren't properly calked, leaked, causing wet clothing and bedding, which was becoming a frequent harassment. Mary Walker's wagon tongue gave way to the pull of the oxen attempting to cross the bog. Working waist deep in water, Griffith Johns repaired the damage.

"When we make camp tonight, Griffith, I'll wash your muddy trousers," Mary offered, as he led the oxen out of the slough.

The next day the trains were confronted by several Indians at yet another bad slough. The Indians had constructed a temporary bridge, which the group gratefully used for a toll of fifty cents!.

An early day camp was found at a grassy area, sorely needed for the complaining livestock. Time was also needed for airing clothing and bedding, as well as other needed maintainence. Enoch Walker arrived in camp, late afternoon, after spending the day searching for a missing ox.

Around the campfire, that evening, the conversation turned to the future, when, and if, they all made it to Oregon.

"I understand a new settlement has started at the southern end of the Rogue River Valley," Cortez commented. "Maybe we can find some suitable farm land in that area."

Nathaniel interjected, "We need to find sufficient land for all of us to be together. At my age, I'm not going to be of much help farming, so you boys will need to be close by. With a new town developing, Franklin and I can probably do some survey work."

The conversation continued, with a general concensus that the south valley area should be their starting point, in their search for land.

"That talk of settling in Southern Oregon caused me to start thinking about our new life there. Will there be suitable stores for our needed supplies, and clothes for little Frances? I am really missing our church and social activities. What about schools?" Questions kept flowing from Elizabeth to Cortez, as they lay in bed that night.

"Liz, I have wondered about these things too, but there are so many emigrants arriving in Oregon, some of them will be working on all of this. I just hope there will be sufficient land left for all of our families to homestead!"

The families awoke to an early morning chill, aggravated by a penetrating strong wind. The women, not inclined to fix a hot meal, prepared a quick bread and fruit breakfast, and the group hastened their departure for today's adventure in their travel west. Frequent crossings of streams and sloughs continued throughout the day. Again, they were fortunate in finding bridges for most. Arriving at the Elkhorn River, the group used a ferry to transport the wagons, at a cost of $5.00 each. Swimming the livestock across the dangerous stream was finally accomplished, but not without the loss of several calves, swept away by the relentless current. When the wagon trains were finally across, and ready to continue, Fruit lamented to his brothers,

"That was a costly crossing!"

"If we have many more like that, I just hope we'll have enough money to make it through to Oregon!" Enoch added.

With a pained laugh, John lightened their concerns,

"Well, we could start a new settlement here in this Nebraska territory. We are only three or four days from Council Bluffs!"

145

The rest of the day was filled with complaints from everyone, including the cattle, as the wind added to the misery created by the dusty road. Reaching a grassy area, the cattle refused to go any further. Not an ideal place for camping, the dejected travelers spent the night swatting mosquitoes!

MAY 14, 1853

The morning of the 10th was again chilly, with frost, but without yesterday's wind. During breakfast, two Indians arrived, seeking food.

"Our hunting grounds are no longer home to the buffalo, elk, and antelope. White travelers and trappers have depleted the grass, and slaughtered the animals. Our harvest of corn has been consumed to allow for our long winter survival," one of the Indians complained.

Realizing that there was some truth in his words, and that they were in Indian territory, Franklin replied, "Our cattle have suffered from lack of grass, and we have found little evidence of game. We are in sympathy with your plight." Having said this, he offered them ham, dried beef, bread, and salt. "I'm not sure that was a good idea," Nathaniel questioned his son, as the two Indians departed. "We, likely now, will have more of them show up."

"What should I have done, Dad? Why, it was you and mother that taught me to share with others less fortunate." "Well spoken, Franklin, but I'm not sure, at this point, we are better off than those two Indians!"

Traveling was much better today, with a good road, and no streams to cross. By the end of the day, the wagon trains were eighteen miles closer to Oregon, camped on the prairie, where they found adequate grazing for the livestock. The campers did not fare as well, for there was no firewood to be had. The women tried to cook supper, using dry course grass for fuel. To add to their discomfort, rain started to fall.

The next few days the families continued to make good distances in their travel. Nathaniel's fear of more Indians looking for food, did not materialize, much to Franklin's relief. On the 12th, they were confronted by a group of Indians at Shells Creek, asking for a toll to use the bridge. Franklin refused to pay, stating that the bridge was built by the emigrants. When the Indians left, without any further confrontation, he felt some redemption from the earlier encounter that caused comment by his father.

By the 14th the wagons had reached the ferry at Loup River. Another financially painful toll precluded their crossing, but, instead they elected to ford the river at a suitable spot upstream. Fortunately, the passage was made without any major problem, creating a good feeling among the group for all the precious money saved! The families proceeded west, under a huge thunder cloud that deluged them with torrents of rain, and fierce gusts of wind! Enoch Walker's sleeping wagon cover was blown to shreds. The top of the carriage containing Mrs. Walker, and her daughter, was removed to prevent it from upsetting. They were forced to endure the remaining day's travel without any protection.

After another required fording at Beaver Creek, the wagons suffered further leakage from the high water crossing. By the time they reached camp, everyone, and everything was soaked. Attempting to eat supper in the continuing wind and rain, Mary Walker complained, "I can't stand another stormy night!"

MAY 18,1853

The terrain has become more rolling, with few trees, but more grass for the livestock. The wagon trains forded Cedar Creek on the 15th. The creek was about 100 feet across, but only two feet, or so, deep. No problems were encountered in the crossing. With the lack of trees, firewood became a problem. After traveling some fourteen miles, they camped on the banks of a beautiful lake.

Thunderstorms were again dumping their misery, as the group traveled southwesterly along the north fork of the Loup River. When the river took a turn north, they should be able to ford the shallow stream without too much problem. However, the sandy river bottom caused one of the oxen pulling Nathaniel and Mary's wagon, to flounder.

"Jackson, can you help my ox get out of that quicksand?" Nathaniel yelled. In so doing, Jackson was trampled by the ox, as the huge beast lunged forward. Nathaniel, handing the reins to Mary, jumped into the river to help. "Are you badly hurt, Jackson?"Nathaniel anxiously shouted, as he hurried to help him. Spitting water and sand, Jackson grasped Nathaniel's arm.

"When I slipped, trying to pull him loose, that damned ox stepped on my leg with all of his weight. It might be broken."
With Jackson leaning heavily on Nathaniel's shoulder, they struggled to shore.

"Bring the wagon on Mary," her husband called. "Jackson's injured, and we need to get him out of this awful downpour!"

Meanwhile, some of the other oxen teams were bogged down in the stream. Other teams were brought to rescue them. In spite of all the confusion, aggravated by the storm, all of the wagons and livestock eventually made it to the other side. Exhausted, and drenched, they sought shelter at a nearby camp. The last of their firewood provided some relief, as they managed to cook supper, and dry out around the fire.

Sporadic rain continued the next day, as the wagons trudged on. The sticky, humid weather caused short tempers, with sharp words answering the smallest of irritations. The excitement and enthusiasm prevalent earlier, had turned into doubt and misery. Jackson was hurt, and Knight was down with scurvy. What would happen to them next!

Despite this gloomy attitude, the group ended the day with more miles behind them than any other. The twenty two miles they traveled left them camped at a rain swollen creek too high to ford. Spirits were not enhanced by a cold supper, with no wood to burn.

Unable to ford Prairie Creek, Cortez offered a suggestion.

"If we remove the wagon bed, we can float our provisions across. Then the oxen can pull the rest of the wagon across from the other side." The idea worked!

More challenging creeks were forded as the day progressed. The effort and ingenuity required seemed to boost their morale. This was dampened, however, when another cold supper resulted from the lack of fuel! That evening, Enoch and Fruit watched over the cattle, as the animals filled their bellies with the abundant grass!

MAY 21, 1853

The camp awakened with delight, to find the prairie covered with frost! Finally, the thunderstorms, and humid days were over! Now, if they could just find some firewood, or even buffalo chips, along the trail, the day could end with a hot meal!

The ferry crossing at Wood River was deluged with wagon trains waiting. It was too late for further travel by the time both the Myer and Walker trains were ferried across. They made their camp near several others, bordering the river. Again they were subjected, with the absence of fire wood, to another cold dinner.

Confronting a neighboring camper, Fruit angerly exclaimed,

"That's my revolver, in my holster, hanging from your waist!" Snapping his bull whip, Fruit threatened "Unstrap it and hand it back!" Instead, the man reached for the gun, which was a big mistake! The whip snapped his wrist, causing the revolver to fall. Quickly, Fruit recovered it. "Now, I am also missing a sack of flour. Is that it?" he demanded, pointing to the sack inside the man's tent.

"I bought that sack of flour at Kanesville."

"You are a liar and a thief!" Fruit seethed, shoving him toward the sack. "Now take it back to where you found it."

After the flour was returned, Fruit marched the thief back to the Wood River ferrmen.

"I caught this culprit stealing from me," Fruit advised. "We've had a lot of complaints of stealing from other emigrants," one of the ferry operators replied. "We're glad you caught him. Just leave him with us, and we'll take care of him."

"What do you think they will do to him?" Mary questioned her husband, upon his return to camp.

"Well, the closest jail is at Ft. Kearney, which is a hard day's ride from here. Since we'll be passing by there in a couple of days, I offered to testify. The ferrymen said it wouldn't be necessary."

Notwithstanding this rocky start, the group managed to travel fifteen miles before making camp. A small herd of antelope was spotted, grazing on the prairie grass, off in the distance. Not only a good fisherman, Griffith Johns was an expert hunter. Buffalo chips made perfect coals for a barbeque feast!

The women were excited, and eager to shop for needed provisions, upon reaching Ft. Kearney. The fort was established for the protection of the emigrants, as well as a trading center. The families had not seen anything but wilderness since leaving Council Bluffs over two weeks ago.

While the ladies were involved with shopping at the trading post, the men took advantage of the barber shop, with haircuts, shaves, and hot baths.

Mrs. Janet Powell, wife of the post commander, Col. L.E. Powell, was also engaged in shopping for supplies for the Officers Saturday night social. Observing the Myers and Walkers, particularly the younger, single women, she mused, "perhaps I should invite them to the party. Some of our single men should be delighted to have the monotony of this isolated post spiced up by the presence of these pretty ladies."

Introducing herself to the group, with her usual friendly greeting, she did, indeed, invite them to the party.

"Thank you so much, Mrs. Powell, but we are traveling emigrants, and we are not prepared for parties and such," Elizabeth Myer responded. Seventeen year old Sarah Myer eagerly interjected. "Why, we have all the clothes we own, including party dresses, stored in our trunks!"

"Please understand that we live very lonely lives here, far from the comforts found in the U.S." Mrs. Powell pointed out. "You, who travel through here, provide an outlet for us that is so important. Please come." "We have young children, including my six-month old baby. We can't just leave them at our campsite," Elizabeth argued.

"Now don't you worry about that, Liz," Mary Myer replied.

"Nathaniel and I are too old to be out partying. We'll be happy to stay in camp with the children."

"Then its settled!" Janet Powell proclaimed. "We will be expecting you around seven, and if any of your group plays an instrument, please help us with the entertainment."

The evening was a huge success, boosting the morale of everyone. Sarah was thrilled, dancing with handsome, young officers, as were her older sisters. The Myer and Walker couples also enjoyed the dancing, as well as interesting discussions with the post residents. Griffith Johns was invited to play folk songs on his harmonica, which was a treat for the hosts. Carriages were provided by Col. Powell, for the short distance to their campsite. On the way, Fruit, in an amorous mood, confided to Mary, "You were the prettiest girl there, causing me to realize how much I love you, and how little I show it. Tonight, I want to hold you in my arms, loving you in every erotic way, until morning comes, or we fall asleep, exhausted!"

"Oh, Fruit, my handsome lover; I want you so!

JUNE 1, 1853

The next several days found the Myer/Walker families making good mileage, plodding along the trail adjacent to the Platte River. A wide, shallow, and muddy stream, it was often described as too thin to plow, and too thick to drink!

By May 23rd the wagon trains had traveled halfway through the Nebraska territory, two hundred and fifty miles west of the Missouri River, averaging fifteen miles per day. They were now in buffalo country. Nathaniel wrote in his diary, "Clear Morning. Signs of Buffaloe. Seen none of the animals yet. Upon examining some of the guides, we are about 244 miles from the Missouri River. Made 20 miles. Encamped. Buffolo chips to cook."

Bluffs along the river, required the trail to traverse through sloughs and heavy bottom land. With wagons mired in mud, traveling became tedious. Still, they were managing better than twenty miles each day. Another heifer was left behind, unable to keep up through the muddy bogs. The road remained difficult, as they continued through the bluffs, toward Chimney Rock.

Trees gradually disappeared, replaced by sagebrush and prairie grass. Mary Myer noticed this, sitting beside her husband, as they trudged along the trail. "Look ahead, Nathan, there isn't a tree in sight!" "Yeah, I know. Horn's Guide states that we have seen the last timber for the next two hundred miles!"

Stormy days aggravated the road conditions. Finally, in a chuck hole, buried in the muddy ruts, Nathaniel's springed wagon came to an end. Damaged beyond repair, the Myer men salvaged the wood for fuel, and left the iron. From now on the bumpy, and springless ox wagon would be "home" for the elder Myers! They were now, on the 29th of June, three hundred and seventy two miles west of the Missouri, and sixteen hundred miles from their destination, the Rogue River

Valley, in Southern Oregon.

"I just can't get him to go any further, Enoch," John Walker explained to his older brother, as he coaxed the big bull they had purchased in Iowa.

"Damn! He's sired such good stock, I hate to lose him." Well, stay with him, while he rests for a while, John. We'll be stopping, in a couple of hours, for the night. If you can't get him to move after an hour or so, just leave him, and catch up with us." Reluctantly, John was forced to leave the bull, and head for camp. Another animal was lost to the rigor of the trail. The brushy land was causing sores on the tender feet of the young calves. When the caravan stopped for lunch the next day, Fruit and Enoch Walker discussed the problem. Fruit suggested,

"Maybe, we should treat the infected area with antiseptic balm, and then try to seal it with our calking material."

"Well, if we don't do something, we, for sure, are going to lose them," his brother agreed. "It would help if we could drive the cattle around these brushy parts of the trail. I'll scout ahead of the herd, and try to steer you away from the brush." The treatment, along with Enoch's guidance appeared to help.

Everyone cheered as Chimney Rock came into view. It was the most famous landmark on the Oregon Trail. The tall spire, rising out of the hearth-shaped base, creates the appearance of a gigantic chimney looming above the harsh terrain. That evening, the first day of June, 1853, they camped, with it in sight. Campfire conversation centered on the awesome formation, as it slowly disappeared in the night.

Later, using the dim light of his lantern, and sitting in his chair in the wagon, Nathaniel wrote in his diary,

"W.June 1st. Cloudy & some rain. Some of the calfs' feet are giving out. The boys are doctoring them at noon. Made 25 miles. Road good. Camped 3 miles east

of Chimney Rock, 440 miles west of the Missouri."

JUNE 9, 1853

Following their exiting day at Chimney Rock, the trains trekked another twenty miles, camping near Scotts Bluff, another well know landmark. They had been gradually gaining in elevation since leaving the Missouri River, and were now at 3,900 feet, some 3,000 feet higher. While the terrain, generally, is still flat, outcroppings, such as Scotts Bluff are scattered about, forewarning travelers of the mountains to come!

Weeks of wearisome travel, pulling the heavy wagons through muddy ruts, began to show on the dependable oxen. One, obviously unable to continue without resting, was sold for $100. The rest of them were not in much better condition, and the long haul up the Laramie Mountains lay ahead.

Trees were now softening the landscape, as the group approached Ft. Laramie. Indian Villages also added to Nature's portrait. Stopping for a lunch break at the fort, some of the men decided to inquire about fresh oxen. "We operate sort of an animal library here," the stableman laughed. "You can have some of the oxen brought in by earlier emigrants, in exchange for yours. All we charge is the pasture rent and feed during their stay here, plus a little for our time and trouble." After a little more bargaining, the exchange was made! Meanwhile, at the wagons, a group of Indians arrived, offering moccasins and dried buffalo meat.

"Our money and supplies are limited", Dolly Myer explained. "Some freshly baked bread and dried fruit is all we can spare." The women and children sorted through the moccasins, finding the right size, agreeing to a loaf of bread for each pair. The buffalo meat and dried fruit were similarly exchanged.

On the trail again, Dolly described the trade with the Indians, to Franklin. "We, at least, have shoes for the women and children, for hiking through the mountains, and sufficient meat to last until Ft. Bridger," she concluded.

After traveling twenty-three miles that day , the weary families camped, wondering how they would handle trudging through the snow capped mountains, now plainly in sight. Heading into the mountains, the next morning, the group reluctantly paused as they passed by Register Cliff. Some of the children had heard that the emigrants carved their names on the soft sandstone outcropping.

"It is just not right, to deface mother natures work for no reason, other than to carve your names on it," Nathaniel scolded. "Besides, we have no time for such nonsense." It was the only time on the trail that he exercised his patriarchal authority.

Surprisingly, the Laramie Mountains were not that difficult to cross. For the most part, they traveled over good roads. In one bad spot, Enoch's wagon wheel collapsed, requiring him to backtrack about six miles, to retrieve a wheel from an abandoned wagon. By the 9th of June, the group had made it through the Laramies, and were camped in the high desert to the west, along the N. Platte River.

JUNE 10, 1853

"This thunderstorm is bound to·spook the cattle, Mary," Fruit Walker,
concerned, awakened his wife. "I had better lend the guard a hand, or we will
have livestock scattered everywhere." "Not again!" Mary complained. "Please
don't leave me alone with this awful thunder and lightning! What if my tent
collapses again in this gale?"

"Now Mary, just calm down. This storm will soon pass, and I'll be back.
Otherwise, I'll be out all night, rounding up the cattle."

Fruit, astride his horse, found the frightened herd threatening to stampede.
Fortunately, most of the other men joined in, allowing them to keep the animals
contained.

Meanwhile, wind gusts flattened every tent in the camp! A lightning flash
momentarily turned night into day, exposing the terrified women and children
scurrying for shelter. The inevitable, crackling, rolling thunder followed,
deafening their screams, as they huddled together under the cover of the wagons.

The thunderstorm did not deter the group from an early start, as the wagons
headed west, blessed with clear skies and the fresh morning air. Griffith Johns
brought his horse beside Mary's wagon. "You look pretty well recovered from last
night, Mary," was his greeting.

"Thanks to you, Griffith. You are my angel!" While they were chatting, the
caravan came to a halt at the campsite of another emigrant.

"My wife is inside the tent, with bad labor pains," the emigrant advised.
"Do you have a doctor or a midwife in your group?" he questioned Nathaniel and
Mary.

"I've birthed nine children, and have helped deliver dozens more," Mary
replied, as the expectant father assisted her from the wagon. "We'll need

159

boiling water, and clean towels. Entering the tent, Mary found the wife in obvious distress. "How long have you been in labor, dear?"

"I don't know," she gasped in pain. "Please help me!"

Sensing that something was not right, Mary gently placed her hands under the baby's head, and discovered the problem. With the umbilical cord tightly wrapped around its tiny throat, the baby was dead.

With his sons' help, Nathaniel dug a small grave, under a shade tree, just off the trail. Franklin tied two branches to form a cross, while Cortez gathered some rocks to hold it. Quietly, Mary told the couple, crying in each others arms, as she tried to comfort them, "My husband has made a grave for your baby, and my sons have built a cross." Mary took the baby cuddled in their arms. Slowly, with tears in her eyes, she left, hearing the mournful sobs of the distraught mother. That night Nathaniel wrote in his diary, " Wind blowed down all the tents last night. Made 21 miles. Part of the road sandy and heavy. Camped close to the river. Wood, water and grass plenty. We passed a tent in which a still babe was born; the mother was doing well."

JUNE 14, 1853

The 11th of June the families found many other emigrants camped along the trail, creating an overgrazed area that would plague them for days. Realizing that the lack of grass might cause the loss of livestock, they purchased sacks of grain, as the train passed by the Glen Rock trading post. Later in the day, at Ft. Caspar, the women restocked their dwindling food supply, buying flour, sugar, coffee, and dried beef. Cortez was able to sell an ox, that was lame, for $18.00.

On June 13th, while traveling at a high elevation, through some bluffs, Franklin discovered a huge snow bank about a half a mile ahead of the train. As the wagons approached, Franklin called, "How about some snow ice cream for lunch?" In addition to the snow ice cream, the children made snow forts, seeking them for cover as snowballs flew. After yesterday's tragedy, the snow provided a welcome outlet for relieving their depression. In spite of the long lunch break, the group traveled fourteen miles, before camping along a sparkling, clear stream called Greasewood Creek. Taking advantage of its clarity, the women washed the children's clothing, dirtied from their outing in the snow. Early morning heavy frost froze the drying garments, requiring additional use of scarce wood for fire to get them dry.

"That must be Independence Rock," Nathaniel yelled, from his wagon, to some of his family, who were walking along the trail. Another landmark, the large formation acquired its name from a group of travelers passing by on July 4th, Independence day! Situated about halfway along their Oregon Trail journey, emigrants felt the need to be here by the 4th of July, not only to celebrate, but to reach their destination before the disastrous winter storms would engulf them. Although a harder rock, than Register Cliff, the formation was also

161

graffitied by hundreds of carvings.

Following along the Sweetwater River, the caravan arrived at a bridge crossing. Having no other choice, the toll of $3.00 per wagon was paid. The livestock swam across without any difficulty.

The river passes through a gap in the rocky bluffs, so narrow that the trail is forced to circumvent it. The formation is called Devils Gate; probably so named by earlier travelers and trappers. Here, in this picturesque setting, the group made camp for the night. Describing Devils Gate, Nathaniel wrote,

"Camped near Devils Gate, a curiosity indeed. A branch of Sweetwater passes through a small gap of rock, which are between three and four hundred feet. I was mistaken in saying that a branch of Sweetwater passed through the Gate: the whole river passes through. We were realy in a salaratus rigion; the women gathered gallons of it, apparently as pure as that that is sold in market in the States."

"Franklin, the wagon's tipping over!" Dolly screamed, as they were attempting to ford a branch of the Sweetwater. Hearing his wife's call, Franklin turned his horse, as he watched the wagon lurch on its side, with the ox team thrashing in the current. "All of you men get over here quick!" he called, fearing for his wife and children trapped inside of the overturned wagon. The men dove into the partially submerged wagon, rescuing the frightened occupants.

"Come on Dolly, I'll get you to shore," Franklin shouted above the roar of the river, while pulling her out of the wagon, and into his arms.

"What about our children, and all of our belongings?" Dolly cried out in sobbing, hysterical shrieks! Trying his best to console her, Franklin answered,

"The kids have all gotten out, and they look OK! I'll help them get the wagon to shore." When the children, choking with water, and covered with mud, fell crying at their mother's side, she gathered her composure, asking,

"Oh my God, my precious ones; are you all right?"

Dolly and Franklin surveyed the salvaged wagon with grim feelings. The wagon contents were scattered from one end to the other, soaked with muddy water. The lantern was shattered, books were ruined, and all the clothing was stained with the reddish clay of the river bottom. The wagon cover was also stained, and the supporting hoops were bent askew. In addition, a wagon wheel had collapsed, and the yokes were damaged. Feeling resentment and anger, Dolly railed,

"Everything we own is ruined. The children and I could have drowned! I'm so cold and wet, and my hair is caked with mud."

After making the needed wagon repairs, the trains trudged on, along the Sweetwater, which they would follow to the continental divide. Camping early, they found a suitable spot beside a pretty stream flowing into the river.

With all of the families' help, Dolly and Franklin were able to wash the mud stained clothing and bedding and clean out the debris from the wagon. Laying in bed, the next morning, Dolly commented to her husband. "It was very thoughtful for everyone to help us. I feel so much better today, Franklin. You are a fine husband and father. You are my love, and I will be with you, wherever you choose to go. "Dolly, I know this is difficult and dangerous. I love you, and thank you for your love. Together, we will find a new life in Oregon, that will be worth the challenge and hardships that this long journey requires."

Feeling the strength of his arms around her, she stroked the back of his neck, and pulled his body to hers.

Dolly's wagon was a sorry sight, with it's stained, tilted cover, mud caked sides and squeaking bent wheel. Franklin felt embarrassed that his pretty wife and handsome children were its occupants. Furthermore, South Pass was just a few days ahead, and with the wagon in such poor condition, he questioned that it could make it. His chance to replace it came the next day, when they arrived at a wagon supply trading post operated by a fur trader.

"I take wagons like yours, and restore them," the trader advised. "Most of the trains that come by, have damaged wagons, so I do real well. Right now, though, I have several wagons on hand, and don't need any more."

"We would buy two of your wagons, and some ox teams, if you would give us a trade for this wagon, and some of our tired oxen," Franklin offered. After some bargaining, the trade was made. Abandoning one of his worn out wagons several days earlier, Fruit Walker took the extra wagon, and a team of oxen.

That evening, at camp, Franklin helped Dolly set up housekeeping in the new wagon. He was relieved that his wife had recovered from that terrible accident.

June 19, 1853

"About a foot and one-half below the surface, there is a bed of clear ice that can be found any time of the year," Nathaniel quoted from his guide book, when the caravan arrived at Ice Slough. A sharp wind was blowing, as it frequently does, in this high sage plain. The tundra-like soil provides an insulation that keeps the frozen spring from thawing. There are no trees or bushes; just sagebrush .

Cortez and Fruit dug through the topsoil until their shovels struck the icy surface below. Depleted water kegs were filled with chunks of ice, which would provide welcome ice water for satisfying their thirst.

A few miles beyond Ice Slough the group found two small ponds, bubbling water from springs below.

"This pool is just right for a hot bath!" Sarah Myer eagerly exclaimed. Most everyone, donned with swim suits, frolicked in the ponds; first the hot one, and then cooling off in the cold pool. What a pleasant relief, the break provided, from the monotony of travel through this, seemingly, endless desert sage.

Gradually climbing towards South Pass, the trains began passing patches of snow. The parched cattle balked at each spot, trying to quench their thirst.

"Lets keep our eyes open for a camp close to a snow bank, Fruit," Cortez suggested to his brother–in–law.

"Yeah, if we don't, this herd will scatter tonight, looking for water."
That evening they were rewarded, not only with a snow bank, but with enough grass to keep the animals contented.

Following a long twenty-two mile trek the next day, they camped within five miles of the continental divide, still in that high desert terrain that makes a twenty-mile swath, through South Pass, across the Rocky Mountains.

JUNE 23, 1853

The caravan paused at the South Pass summit, as everyone gathered to look out to the west. The climb to the top was accomplished without any of the feared disasters associated with crossing the awesome Rocky Mountains. Their elevation was seven thousand,five hundred feet; by far the highest altitude attained by any of them. Nathaniel Myer, facing the strong westerly wind that caused tears in his one good eye, placed him arm around Mary's waist, and tightly held her.

"Mary, we are now standing on the great divide, looking into the territory of Oregon!

That evening the trains camped beside Little Sandy creek; the first stream flowing to the west. After fording the creek the next morning, they followed it until they reached the confluence of the Big Sandy two days later. Deciding that it was too deep to ford, without adequate preparation, the families camped beside the river.

Huddled around the campfire, fighting the wind chill of the frigid night, the company conversation centered around their progress west.

"It's been three months since we left our homes in Iowa, and I figure that we are over halfway through," Cortez apprised the group. "Sometimes its hard for me to realize that we have crossed the Rockies, and are in Oregon territory."

Preparing for the river crossing, the wagon beds were raised. Bedding and clothing were secured safely from any water leakage. One by one, the wagons forded the dangerously deep stream. Franklin, trying to avoid another accident, drove his wagon team, with Dolly and their children on board, slowly through the swift current, safely to the other side. Heaving a sigh of relief, he muttered to himself, "I'll be damned glad when we finally have crossed the last of all of these treacherous streams!" One of the worst, yet to come, the Green River, would be reached tomorrow.

"Mother, I don't feel good," Minerva complained .

"Neither do I. Do you have an upset stomach, like mine?" Temperance asked.

"Yes, and I'm awfully hot. Can you get me a drink of water?"

Temperance called to her mother, Mary Myer, who was busy preparing breakfast. "Minerva and I are both sick at our stomach, and seem to have a fever."

As Mary tended to them, she related, "Three in the Walker train also have stomach aches. You must have all eaten something that had spoiled. All that you can do is rest, and drink lots of water. You stay in bed, and I'll drive the team for you today."

Food poisoning was a very serious concern for all of the wagon trains. Everyone eating the contaminated food could become sick and disabled at the same time, leaving no one to carry on. Fortunately, so far at least, most of the group had no symptoms, and participated in sterilizing the cooking ware, dishes, and utensils in boiling water. All of the perishable provisions were examined, and questionable items were discarded. Getting a late start, the caravan headed, along the Big Sandy, for their rendezvous with the Green River. After 16 miles of bumpy road, the sick ones begged to stop. They were still six miles from the river.

With a clear, warm day, the families got an early start, and arrived at the Green River by mid-morning. The livestock forded the stream , with all, but three, drowned, yearling calves, safely across by noon. It was not uncommon for this crossing to take two or three days, with a much greater loss of cattle.

By afternoon the wind was too strong to risk ferrying the wagons.

"Have your wagons ready to go by sunrise," the ferryman requested.

Another beautiful day blessed the families, as they began ferrying the wagons across the dangerous Green River. The wagon carrying Nathaniel and Mary Myer was the first, followed by the Fruit and Mary Walker wagon, with Mary on board. Fruit was tending the herd that had crossed yesterday. In the middle of the river, where the current was swift, the barge broke loose from the line, causing it to rapidly float downstream. One of the ferrymen attempted to hold the ferry, catching his foot on the line, but was pulled overboard. Watching the incident from shore, Griffith Johns spurred his horse into the stream. Reaching into the water, Griffith grabbed the ferryman's outstretched hand, and shouted, "Hold on, while I pull you over to my horse!" In so doing, he was pulled into the swirling current. Fighting for his own survival, Griffith released his grip, separating the two, as they were swept downstream. Spotting an island that had beached the Walker wagon barge, Griffith spent his last bit of strength to reach it.

Meanwhile, the terrified Mary Walker screamed for help as the wayward barge rocked and turned in the wild river, before crashing onto the shore of the island. As she scrambled out, the struggling Griffith called. "Help me ashore, Mary. I don't have the strength to fight this current, as his fingers dug into the sandy beach. Pulling him on to shore, Mary fell backward, causing Griffith to land, clumsily, on top of her. Exhausted, he made no effort to move, as she cried in his arms.

A line was stretched from the island to the western bank, making it possible to ferry the barge and cargo safely to shore. Griffith recovered his horse, but the ferryman was found, caught by a branch, face down in the water, drowned.

"We've been ferrying here for years; ain't lost a single man, and now we got two of them to bury," one of the ferrymen lamented to Fruit, as they were getting the wagon back on the trail. "Yesterday, an emigrant fell off the ferry boat and drowned. We'll be burying him today, and I recon we will do the same with Josh."

A member of the drowned emigrant's train, being a Baptist preacher, led the burial service for both the victims. Most of the Myer/Walker party attended.

The reverend ended with a sad but sage prayer. "Lord, you have taken these souls away from this harsh and unforgiving land, that they may dwell in your house forever! Help those of us left, to gain strength, and remain steadfast in your service. Guide us safely through the challenges that remain before us. Amen. "

JUNE 28, 1853

Summer storms, usual for this high country, alternated with clear, cold
weather for the next several days. The storms frequently brought snow, with
banks of it all along the trail.

"The snow banks will provide the water we need, as well as for the
livestock," Fruit offered, as the group discussed their route west from the
Green River. "I think we should take the Sublette cut-off."

"The guide book doesn't recommend it because of the terrain, and the lack of
water," Nathaniel countered. "You do make a point, using the snow for water, and
we will save precious time. So I guess I'd be for it. Pros and cons continued,
causing Elizabeth Myer to furiously work on her neglected quilt.

"You must be worried again, Liz; working on that quilt like that," her
mother-in-law observed.

"Mother Mary, whenever the men talk like they are doing now, I start
wondering what is going to happen to us. I just have to keep busy doing this, or
I'll become a nervous wreck!"

"Well, which route do you think we should take, Liz?"

"To me, the choice is plain. We should take the one that is the safest.
Besides, if we take the cut-off, we will bypass Ft. Bridger. Dolly will be upset
about that. Franklin promised her she could buy some new clothes there, to
replace the ones that got stained when their wagon tipped over in the river.
After finally making a decision, the families headed their wagons on to the
Sublette trail.

Fruit Walker was right about using the snow for water, but on the second
day, where the trail was treacherous, Mary's wagon overturned. Fortunately, the
snow bank prevented much damage, except to Mary's already frayed nerves!

Steep terrain, with ravines, chuck holes, and the rocky trail of the
Sublette Cut-off, made travel difficult and dangerous. At one point an oxen team
bolted in fear, pulling the bouncing wagon until an axle cracked on a protruding
rock. Dolly Myer was the terrified driver. Franklin, behind, tending the
cattle, galloped his horse in pursuit. Reaching the frightened team, he grabbed
the reins, and with the help of the dragging axle, brought them to a halt.
Franklin immediately jumped onto the wagon to help his distraught wife. Sobbing
in his arms, she screamed, "We never should have taken this awful route. Our
new wagon is now broken, and we still have miles to go. What on earth are we
going to do!"

"Dolly, don't be hysterical! I'm just thankful that you were not hurt!"
After comforting her as much as he could, Franklin surveyed the damage to the
axle. He felt Dolly was probably right about taking the cut-off. They were days
away from any kind of civilization, out in this wild, rocky, desolate desert.
Using balling wire, and iron rods, Franklin temporarily repaired the axle.

The morning of the 30th, the caravan reached Hams Fork. The stream, at the
bottom of a steep rocky ravine, required the wagons to be lowered by ropes, and
then double teamed up the trail on the other side. The fording was slow and
tedious. The tense feeling that gripped the group, caused short tempers, and
harsh words. Franklin's repaired axle snapped in the crossing, and was beyond
any further fixing.

" There was an abandoned wagon we passed yesterday." Franklin remembered.

"Maybe I can salvage an axle. The rest of you go on to camp."

Nathaniel and Mary stayed with the damaged wagon, until Franklin finally
returned. After repairs were made, they reached camp well after dark.

JULY 4, 1853

The families awakened to the warmth of a sunny summer day, after a drenching thunderstorm during the night. Sage brush had to suffice for cooking oatmeal, and frying bacon and bread for breakfast.

The terrain continued to be rough and rocky, as the wagons bounced along the Sublette cut-off. After trekking sixteen miles, the group reached Smith Fork. Finding a suitable campsite, with plenty of water, grass, and sage, they decided to wait until morning before crossing the river. The wagonmaster of another train joined the families that evening, after vainly searching for missing livestock. The warm evening, along with the knowledge that they were through the worst part of the Sublette trail, helped to create a much improved morale. In honor of their guest, a special dinner was prepared, followed with a songfest around the sage brush campfire. The dinner included another mess of trout caught by Griffith Johns from the accommodating stream.

"Griffith, would you mind teaching me how to catch a fish?" Mary queried, as she was filling her water bucket, close by.

"The crickets, that I use for bait, are harder to catch than the fish!" he laughingly replied. "I put a small hook on my line; just big enough to be covered up by the cricket, and then I tie on a sinker about a foot and a half above the hook. Then I cast out just above that hole over there, and let the weight sink to the bottom. The current drags the line into the hole, letting the bait bounce along where the fish are. Here, you take the pole and try it. When you feel a little nibble, quickly set the hook with a short jerk on the pole."

"I've got one!" Mary excitedly exclaimed, reeling the fighting trout to shore.

Smith's Fork has a toll bridge, with a charge of $2.00 per wagon.

"Considering the time and risk involved in fording the stream, I think we are ahead to pay the toll," Cortez suggested to Fruit Walker.

"Yeah, your are probably right, Cortez. We could pay for several tolls for the cost of one wagon damaged in fording, and we will be across, and on our way, long before we could ford it."

Both wagonmasters agreeing, the toll was paid, and shortly they were on the trail again. Before long the caravan arrived at another toll crossing. Not as long a bridge, they were able to negotiate a fee of $0.10 per wagon. The final toll of the day was $25.00 for the entire train, at Thomas Creek, where, after a twenty-mile day, they camped for the night. In spite of the three toll crossings, the good road was a welcome relief from the terrible terrain traveled the past few days.

Another eight miles of up and down steep gullies, aggravated by the first fog since the Missouri River, confronted the wagon trains, causing them to quit for the day after reaching Bear River.

On this summer 4th of July, The caravan, now back on the Oregon trail, had successfully traversed the Sublette Cut-off! Around the sage brush campfire that night, the children celebrated Independence day with sparklers and firecrackers!

JULY 5, 1853

"Oh, look at the water spouting out of that big rock!" young George Myer exclaimed, when the trains arrived at Soda Springs. By the time he reached the geyser, all that remained was a small hole, of bubbly water flowing over the surface of the boulder. On his hands and knees, George attempted to taste it, just as the water spouted again. He laughed, wiping his face, "This water really tastes funny!" By then, the rest of the kids had arrived, with their parents not far behind.

Soda springs was a curiosity, mentioned in guide books, and diaries, stemming from the effervescent water. Some described it as "having a beer-like taste." The comments from this group varied from "invigorating" to "noxious!" None the less, corked bottles were filled with the "bubbly," to be used for "medicinal" purposes! The reason uncertain, one of the Myer cows, quite suddenly, died, later on that day! Nathaniel, keeping his suspicion to himself, pondered, "I'll bet that cow drank too much of that gaseous water!"

Camped a few miles west of the Fort Hall road, the families enjoyed another sagebrush campfire.

"The Hudspeth Cut-off to Raft River is a lot shorter than going by way of Fort Hall," Nathaniel observed, studying his guide book. "Do we need to replenish our supplies? The guide doesn't show any trading post on the cut-off, nor on the California and Applegate trails."

Looking over his father's shoulder, Cortez surveyed the guide map.

"Looks like we could save several days, traveling the cut-off, so I'd be for taking it," he suggested. The consensus of the men favored the cut-off, with the women, disappointed in missing Fort Hall, reluctantly agreeing.

July 6, 1853

"Maybe we made a mistake by taking this cutoff," Cortez wondered as he
gazed at the rugged and rocky road through the mountains ahead. "We camped
without any water last night, and now we're faced with crossing these barren
buttes on that terrible trail."

"Looks pretty bad doesn't it," Nathaniel agreed. "That appears to be the
steepest grade we've encountered so far."

"We can double team the wagons to climb the mountain, but going down the
other side is going to require ropes and strong oxen," Fruit observed, as the
men discussed the dangerous descent.

Tediously, the wagons trekked up the treacherous trail. A wagon breaking
loose would be disastrous. All, but the wagon drivers, walked, fearing what
would happen should they be trapped in a run-away wagon. The summit provided a
panorama of the terrain ahead. The road stretched straight down, a mile or so,
to the canyon below. Another train could be seen, resting along the stream
flowing through the narrow valley, before attempting the ascending road beyond.
Breaking the tension created by anticipation of the descent, John Walker spurred
his horse. "First one down to the creek gets to go swimming!"

A yoked oxen team was tied to the rear of each wagon, to take the pressure
off the driving team. One by one the wagons safely arrived at the welcome stream
below. The livestock then arrived, filling their parched bodies with gulps of
the precious water.

"Oh, Mercy!" Mary Myer screamed, as she saw a wagon, from the train
ahead, tumbling and crashing down the mountain side. The driver, a young father,
was found, still alive, under the smashed remains. The train had begun the
ascent of the next bluff when the accident occurred. Others, in the group,

managed to carry the injured man to one of the wagons. His wife put his head in her lap, while he moaned, as only the dying do, in semi-consciousness.

"We were going to have such a good life together - - - raising our family in Oregon. - - - I'm sorry - - - I love you" - - -.

After digging a shallow grave in the rocky soil beside the trail, a brother gently removed the dead man from the arms of his grieving mate, and buried him in that lonely plot in those formidable mountains.

In spite of the tragic accident, and the perilous travel, the caravan covered a distance of fifteen miles, camping along Shoshone Creek that evening. Before supper, Griffith Johns gathered up the children for a wild strawberry hunt.

"I'll be glad to join you, Griffith, and help find the strawberries", Mary Walker offered.

"That will be great, Mary. Let's grab a couple of buckets, and see if we can fill them before dark."

A short time later they returned with their buckets full. While Mary removed the stems and washed the berries, the other women prepared biscuits, and whipped cream from a freshly milked cow. The strawberry short cake was a delicious treat that helped relieve the stress from a difficult day.

JULY 13, 1853

The next few days found the group continuing the Hudspeth Cut-off that wandered through the mountains, concluding at the Raft River. Warm summer weather prevailed, with the terrain gradually changing from rocky bluffs to grassy hills. At one mountain summit, the rest of the caravan watched as Fruit Walker attempted to descend without the help of ropes. The wagon tipped over, with little damage done. Near sunset, they decided to spend the night at the summit. The following day, with the use of oxen and ropes, all of the wagons safely reached the bottom. On July 12th, the families crossed the east and middle branches of the Raft River, and camped on the West branch. They were now at the end of the Hudspeth cut-off, having reached the California Trail. Cortez became ill during the day, with sharp pains shooting through his body.

"I'm too sick to get up, Liz. Tell Franklin to take over for me," Cortez muttered to his wife that morning.

"There is a doctor in the train ahead of us. If you aren't better by tomorrow, I'll have someone try to bring him here," a concerned Elizabeth replied.

With Cortez in his wagon bed, The caravan traveled seventeen miles to Cedar Creek. Finding plenty of grass and firewood, they set up their camp along the clear, cold stream. George Sturdevant, one of the Myer hired hands, left to find a doctor for the ailing Cortez. Sturdevant returned with the doctor within a couple of hours.

"You will live through this sir, but it will take some time," the doctor advised. "All of your symptoms indicate that you have Scurvy, which is caused by a poor diet. Now, I realize that it is hard to eat right, out here in this wilderness, but try dried fruit and vegetables. Rest, and drink lots of water.

JULY 14, 1853

Too ill to get up, Cortez was forced to spend another traveling day in his wagon bed. The caravan passed by a natural phenomenon of granite rocks that resembled the ruins of an ancient city. Referring to his guide book, Nathaniel called the formation "The Pyramid Circle". A special treat, the children were allowed to play, for a while, among the boulders. The delay was somewhat costly, for they were required to make camp, without grass, fuel, or water, at the foot of a granite mountain too formidable to cross before sunset.

After a cold supper, Fruit and Franklin explored the area in search of feed for the livestock. Griffith Johns, his back resting against a boulder, filled the warm evening air with soul songs on his harmonica. With no wood, there was no campfire that night. Reading a book by the light of a lantern in her nearby tent, Mary Walker enjoyed the background music. Unable to concentrate, she put down her book, and followed the sounds to Griffith.

"Hi Griffith. I heard you playing those sorrowful folk songs. Do you mind if I join you? "

"Hey Mary, I'd be pleased to have your company. Here, sit down, and I'll share this rock with you."

"Thank you, Griffith, but don't let me stop your playing. I do love your music!" Obliging her, Griffith began playing. Abruptly, he stopped.

"What are you doing out here in this desolate country, Mary? You should have a fine home, with children to raise, back in the States. Instead, here you are, sitting with me, listening to my corny tunes, while Fruit is out looking for grass and water for those complaining cows!"

Jumping to her feet, she scolded, "Well, Mr. Johns, if you don't want my company, I'll be off to my tent! "

"Now Mary, don't be that way. Sit back down. You know I want you to stay. It's just that I shouldn't feel" – – –

"Go on, Griffith. You shouldn't feel what?"

"Nothing," he grumbled, and returned to his harmonica.

Mary, back in her tent, waited for Fruit to return.

"I wonder what Griffith was about to say," were her thoughts. "He is such a deep person; and handsome. I can tell he has feelings for me, and I for him. But this is ridiculous! There has never been anyone but Fruit. I'm so confused... Fruit, please come. I need you to hold me, make love to me, and tell me everything will be all right."

JULY 18, 1853

Double teaming the wagons, the Caravan safely crossed the granite mountain. Cortez was still bedridden, with little or no improvement in his condition. The rough road aggravated his sore body, as the wagon bounced over rocks and chuck holes. Some of the oxen became lame, pulling the heavy wagons up and down the mountain, their hooves slamming into sharp stones littering the trail.

Finally, after fifteen miles of torturous travel, camp was made along Goose Creek. While the grass for the cattle was poor, the stream provided water, and sagebrush was used for fuel. Fruit Walker again took the livestock on a search for better grass.

"I'm sorry about last night, Mary. Sometimes, it is hard for me to express my feelings," Griffith apologized, while setting up her tent.

"Do you feel like talking some more?" Mary replied. "I would like to finish our conversation."

"Well, if you mean, do I have feelings for you? I guess I do. But I'm not going to mess with you or your marriage to Fruit. He is a good man, and he loves you. If things were different – – – but they aren't! I just want to be your friend, if that's possible."

"Oh, Griffith, I want that too! Outside of Fruit, you are my best friend!" Mary gushed, putting her arms around his neck. He kissed her gently, as he removed her arms. "Then, so be it."

That night, as she lay in bed, Mary mused, "I'm so glad that's settled!"

As the days passed, the rough roads took their toll on the wagons, not to mention the sick Cortez. Wagon wheels were dangerously close to collapsing. Finally the road improved, to the relief of everyone, especially Cortez. On the evening of July 18th, the caravan reached the Thousand Springs.

JULY 24, 1853

"If we continue to have good roads, we should be able to reach the Humboldt
River for our camp tonight," Fruit commented to his younger brother, John.

"I sure hope so, Fruit. I'm startin' to get achy, maybe like Cortez."

"Now don't you get sick and die on me, little brother. I got plans for you,
and further, if anything happens to me, I expect you to take over. Anything
could happen out here in this God forsaken sagebrush desert, and if it does I
want you to promise you will look after Mary; you hear?"

"Nothin's gonna happen to you, Fruit!"

"You hear?"

"I hear ya."

"OK, you better just take it easy today, John. Maybe you'll feel better
tomorrow."

The families made it to Bishop Creek, camping a few miles northeast of its
confluence with the Humboldt.

The trains reached the Humboldt River the next morning, and then continued
along the river for the next several days. Not only was Cortez still down, but
several other men including Griffith, were also ill. Unable to ride, Griffith
was bedridden in Mary's wagon, as they continued to travel along the Humboldt.
When time permitted, she bathed Griffith's feverish body with cool water. Sick
as he was, she noticed that her nursing did arouse him.

Around noon of the 24th, the caravan reached the Greenhorn cut-off. It was
decision time again. A number of the men were ill with food poisoning or scurvy.
Fruit and Enoch Walker met with Nathaniel and Franklin Myer.

Showing the others the guide map, Nathaniel pointed out, "If we take the
cut-off, the stock will be without water all day, and the road meanders over

181

those steep hills. With this hot weather, the road will be dusty. Some of the work horses and oxen might not make it."

Fruit, anxious to reach the Rogue Valley, argued, "We will lose a day if we follow the river. We can camp here on the river, which will give the animals a rest, and then get an early start in the morning." His finger tracing the route, Fruit continued, "If all goes well, we'll be able to reach Maggie Creek fairly early tomorrow evening." Again, the decision was made in favor of the cut-off.

JULY 27, 1853

Nathaniel was on the mark with his concerns about the Greenhorn cut-off. While the group did make it to Maggie Creek the next day, as Fruit projected, the dust was choking, and there was no water for the stock. Nancy, one of the black mares, died, and the oxen were in poor condition. The steep, rough roads further deteriorated the worn out wagons. Enoch Walker lost a wheel from his wagon, but was fortunate in finding a suitable replacement from a wagon left behind by an earlier party. The hot days, and dusty, rocky roads aggravated the condition of the sick ones. Cortez complained to Elizabeth, "I can't breathe with all this dust!" His wife kept bathing his sweating body, trying to reduce his fever, and relieve his pain. Mary Walker did the same with Griffith.

Finally, the evening of the 27th, they arrived back on the Humboldt River. Knowing the disastrous effects of the Greehorn cut-off, a permanently camped party greeted them with offers to purchase the lame and exhausted animals. Frankin sold two of his oxen that were in very poor condition, for a total of $15.00.

While the rest of the ill had recovered, Cortez remained in bed, and Frankin developed the symptoms of scurvy.

"Oh, Franklin, what are we going to do! With Cortez down, you just can't get sick!," Dolly despairingly exclaimed. "That leaves only Papa to lead our train, and he looks so frail."

"I'll be feeling better by tomorrow, Dolly. A bath to get rid of this awful dust, and a good night's sleep is all I need." Franklin feebly offered, trying to console his wife. "I'm just thankful that you and little Frances are well!"

183

JULY 28, 1853

"Griffith, our best bull isn't with the herd." Fruit Walker advised, as they were checking the herd, after supper.

"He was there when we arrived in camp; can't be too far away. I'll check around the river to the east. Why don't you check the other way, and we'll meet back here in a couple of hours or so?"

After an unsuccessful river search, they tried other areas, with no luck. By 3:00 a.m., with no sign of the bull, they decided to give up.

"You better get some sleep, Griffith." Fruit suggested. "I'm going to look around the herd, and then try the river again. That bull was so spent, he may have drowned trying to get a drink. I'll bed down later on, by the cattle, for the rest of the night. You might tell Mary where I am."

"Fruit, is that you?" Mary sleepily asked, startled by the rustle of the tent flap, and the appearance of a form outlined in the dimness of the early morning dawn.

No, Mary it's me. Fruit asked me to tell you that he'll be staying with the cattle the rest of the night. He is pretty worried about that expensive bull that's lost," Griffith replied, sitting down beside her.

Pouting, Mary complained, "Sometimes I think Fruit thinks more about the cattle than he does of me!"

In an effort to break her dark mood, he teased, "That's a fine way to greet me!"

"Oh Griffith, you know you are my angel, my friend! Putting her hands on his face, she pulled him to her, embracing and gently kissing his cheek. His breast felt the warmth of hers, and in the passion, so long withheld, his lips touched hers, as they slumped to her bed.

184

JULY 29, 1853

"Griffith, get the hell out of my tent," Fruit angrily cried! Weak from his
illness and lack of sleep, Griffith had made the fatal mistake of falling asleep
beside Mary.

"Now Fruit, it's not what you think" a startled Griffith argued, as he
scrambled to his feet. "You can see I still am dressed. I came to tell Mary that
you were staying with the herd. She became upset, and I tried to console her. I
was so tired, I just fell asleep!"

Always quick to anger, Fruit lashed him with his whip as they left the tent.
"Get on your horse, and clear out of here. If I ever see you again I'll kill
you!" he shouted, whipping Griffith again and again. Trying to cut the lash,
Griffith unsheathed his hunting knife, only to have it snapped from his hand
with the crack of Fruit's whip. He found the revolver in the saddle bag, as he
reached his horse.

"Stop it, Fruit, or I'll shoot," Griffith threatened, revealing his gun
pointed at him. Infuriated, Fruit raised his whip, as Griffith fired two shots.
Clutching the bloody wound in his belly, Fruit slowly slumped to the ground.

Bleeding profusely from the furious whipping, Griffith crawled onto his
horse, and galloped out of sight in the grey of the early morning.

Mary's screams, and the gun shots brought the rest of the families running.
Holding Fruits head in her lap, she cried, "Oh my darling husband! Are you hurt
bad?

"Oh, Mary, my insides are on fire!

"What happened, Mary," Enoch Walker exclaimed, rushing up to the two.

"Fruit's been shot by Griffith Johns," she sobbed.

"Where's Griffith?"

185

"He left on his horse after he shot my husband!" Mary screamed in anguish.

"Help me get him into the tent" Enoch commanded the arriving group.

"I'm going after a doctor ," John Walker yelled, as he ran for his horse.

After this tragic day, Nathaniel Myer wrote in his diary.

"Clear morning. A contravacy took place just at the point of leaving the camp, between Fruit and one of his men (Griffith John) Fruit, having no weepon, Johns having a revolver and a large knife. In the fray Fruit got the knife. Johns discharged two loads out of his revolver; one took effect on Fruit; the ball entered his groins and lodged somewhere. John Walker starded for a docter; he is not returned. The danger of the wound not ascertained; the pain, however, is great. Johns made his escape, although several of the men were in search of him. It is now nearly sunset; no docter as yet. We remained in camp the day. Poor water for men and beasts."

JULY 31, 1853

"I tried all day to located a doctor, without any luck, Mary. How is Fruit doing?" a concerned John walker asked his sister-in-law. It was 3:00 a.m. the following morning that John returned to tell Mary the bad news.

"He's not doing well at all, John. His pain is so bad!"

"Well I informed some of our men that I was back. They left a few minutes ago, in search of one."

"John, come sit beside me," Fruit feebly called, hearing him talking to Mary outside of his tent. "Don't tell Mary this, but I don't think I'm going to make it. That bullet's torn a hole in my guts.- - - I'm pissin' and throwin' up blood.- - - No doctor's goin' to save me.- - - Take care of Mary like you promised."

"I promise, but don't give up, Fruit. We'll get a doctor soon, and he'll fix you up, good as new!" His words, attempting to rally his brother, fell on deaf ears, as Fruit lapsed into unconsciousness.

"Good thing I got here when I did, or he would have soon expired." The doctor informed the anxious group. "The bullet's too deep to remove, but, with God's will, he might make it. Give him a spoonful of this medicine every two hours. It will help control the bleeding, and ease the pain. Keep the wound clean with these sterile pads. That's all you can do, except wait. The next couple of days are critical."

Mary hovered, tirelessly, over her husband. Trying to strengthen his will to live, she confided, "Fruit, my precious husband, you are my life, and my only love. Please don't leave me alone out here in this desolate place!"

"I'm sorry, Mary.- - - I should have trusted you! - - Instead - - my hot temper"- - - -. At the dim dawn of sunrise, Fruit died in Mary's arms.

Like thousands of pioneers before him, whose hopes and dreams were dashed in death, Fruit Walker was buried that morning, on a rocky knoll overlooking the trail to Oregon. Mary Myer ended the service with a prayer. "Lord, we are tired, and bewildered emigrants, grieving over our loss, knowing we must leave Fruit in this harsh desert land. Our sorrow is softened in our faith that you will make a place for him, where, in the unknown future, we will all be together in your Kingdom of Heaven!"

Mary Walker stood, sobbing, beside the pile of rocks covering her husband's grave, long after the rest had left. Fulfilling his promise, Fruit's brother, John, remained, silently mourning, while tenderly holding Mary in his arms.

Nathaniel's diary entry was short and factual. "Clear morning. Fruit died near sunrise. About 12m we enterred Fruit without a coffin of any kind. Made a vault in the grave and with some boards and willows we covered his body over, and filled up the grave and covered the whole with stone. His grave is about 8 miles wist of Ripple Creek on the left side of the road, on rocky and high knole, with a head-board containing his name, age, and when he died, and the name of his last residence. It was a solomn and heard-renting case."

AUGUST 6, 1853

That evening, John Walker moved his tent next to Mary's. He found her,
quietly weeping, in her tent. "Mary, I know it's hard for you to think about
anything when you're grievin' so, but I need to tell you some things before I go
lookin' for Griffith. Fruit must have felt something, cause a few days ago, he
asked me to take care of you, should anything happen to him. I plan on doing
that, and some day, maybe"- -

"John, I'll never love any man but Fruit, Mary sobbed. "I feel so alone and
empty. Why did this have to happen!" she wailed.

"Well I wish I could bring him back, but I can't, Mary; but I can and will
look after you, as long as you will let me. I'll be leavin' early in the
morning, and it may be awhile before I get back. Try to get some rest now." As
John started to leave, Mary grabbed his hand. "Griffith is not a violent man,
but he is desperate. Don't do anything foolish if you find him. I couldn't bear
losing you too!

"I'll go as far as the Applegate Trail, lookin' for Griffith," John advised
his brother, Enoch.

"You be careful, John. He's bound to be dangerous, knowing he'll be hung if
gets caught. If you're not there, when we get to the junction, look for us on
ahead on the Applegate trail."

With John gone, Fruit dead, and the Myer brothers still down with scurvy,
the families were left with only Enoch and Nathaniel to take charge of the
trains. The next few days the conditions didn't get any better. The trail was
rough, oauoing wheel problems with the wagons. Short on hands, aggravated by
poor grass, the cattle became unruly. Several animals were left along the trail,
dying from starvation. Cortez and Franklin were little improved. Mary grieved.

189

August 9, 1853

On the 7th of August, John Walker returned, finding the trains camped along the Humboldt River about fourteen miles east of the Applegate Trail junction.

"I searched every where along the trail, and asked a lot of questions, but Griffith has just disappeared." he related to Enoch. "I even talked to a group of cattle traders permanently camped at the junction, but they hadn't seen anybody the likes of Griffith. How is Mary doin'?"

"All things considered, she's gettin' along alright. At first she just mourned over the loss of Fruit. Now, she keeps asking if we've heard anything from you. She'll be glad to see you."

"Hi Mary! I'm back." John greeted, finding Mary in her tent. Mary rushed to his outstretched arms. "Oh, John, I've worried about you. Thank God you've returned safely. You remind me so, of Fruit, that it's almost as though you are!"

The following day the group reached the Applegate Trail. From here they would be traveling forty miles, through the arid Black Rock Desert, with no grass or water. Cortez was well enough to negotiate the sale of two cows, that would never make it. He was also able to purchase a light wagon which they used to haul feed for the animals.

John found excuses to spend most of his time with Mary, and they talked about their future in the Rogue Valley.

"We'll file claims on adjacent land, Mary, and I'll build our homes close together. You won't be lonely, I promise."

"If you will plant the crops, and tend to the cattle, John, I'll cook the meals, do the wash, and the household chores. We can spend our evenings together, but the nights will be lonely.

AUGUST 10 – SEPTEMBER 3, 1853

"Enoch, Nathaniel is down with his old gall bladder problem. The ordeal of this trail is just too much for him." Mary Myer advised. "I thought I should tell you, cause he's not able to do anything with the train. Cortez and Franklin aren't much better."

"Well we'll manage somehow. John isn't much help, as he is spending most of his time with your daughter."

"I have noticed that. He certainly has been good to her."

"Just between you and me, I think John has fallen in love with Mary Ann!"

"I've wondered about that too, Enoch. Your brother seems to be such a good man. If it comes to that, I wouldn't mind having him for a son-in-law!"

"Right now, though, we need him to help with the cattle. With no water or grass, they are going to require all the manpower we can muster, Mary."

"I think I know how to get them separated," Mary schemed. "Nathaniel is going to need a lot of help, until he gets over this sick spell. I'll ask Mary Ann to take care of him!" The plan worked, as Nathaniel, a very sick man, required most of his daughter's attention.

August 10th was the last diary entry that Nathaniel was able to make during the rest of the journey. The very short entry indicated this. "Clear day. I am not much better. Made 16 miles. Camped at spring. Rough roads."

The next twenty-three days of travel were the most difficult of the entire trip. Short on water, feed, and manpower, the ragged wagons struggled with rough roads through the Black Rock Desert, and then, the steep Cascade mountains, which required ropes to descend.

Finally, on the 3rd day of September, 1853, the tired, bedraggled, and sick families arrived at their new home in what is now, Ashland, Oregon!

Figure 47　L to R - Sarah (Myer)Rockfellow, B.Franklin Myer, Elizabeth (Myer) Anderson, Mary Ann (Myer)Walker, W. Cortez Myer

Figures 48 and 49

Mary Ann Walker, daughter
of Nathaniel & Mary Myer

John P. Walker with son,
Cassius

Figure 50   Some of the Myer/Walker
train group, a few years
after their journey to Oregon.

Figure 51

A.G. & Sarah (Myer) Rockfellow,youngest daughter of
Nathaniel & Mary Myer, with
son, Alfred

Figure 52   Frances Myer (Billings)
             daughter of W.Cortez &
             Elizabeth Myer

EPILOGUE

The next entry in Nathaniel Myer's diary is dated September 25, 1853. He writes about arriving in the "Rogue River Valey" on the 3rd day of September, 1853. All were in good health, except Nathaniel and his two sons, Cortez, and Franklin. The Hills, Wells, and Fordyces, all prominent pioneers, were mentioned as friends who had already arrived in the valley. Asa Fordyce had been wounded in an Indian attack a few days before the Myer/Walker trains arrived. Although struck by two bullets and an arrow, he survived. Also named was Hugh Smith(possibly a military officer) who was killed in the same raid. Obviously, the emigrants of the valley were still involved with land disputes with the local tribes, as they filed claims, and settled on what, for centuries, had been Indian territory.

Most of the cattle survived the grueling conditions of the long journey, and became the main source of livelihood for the Myer and Walker families. Cortez, in fact became quite prominent, raising Percheron horses, Shetland ponies, and Jersey cattle. Part of the land, including his house and barn, is still owned and occupied by a great grandson of Cortez and Elizabeth.

Apparently, the Myers and Walkers had some difficulty in filing their homestead claims. Nathaniel wrote, "The boys have made their locations for themselves and for me, about 12 miles east of Jacksonville, Jackson County, all in one track. The walkers have made their location about 10 miles west of us in the same valley, in one body. We all have had some difficulties in making our locations, on account of so many land–claimers that do not intend to make it their homes. Some of our and Walkers' land located is claimed by some of those gentries."

The Myer families settled in what is now known as north Ashland and Valley

View areas, while the Walkers chose land southeast of Ashland. Mary Ann Walker did marry her brother-in-law, John P. Walker, but, as near as we can determine, not until February 20, 1855.

Nathaniel immediately started keeping monthly rainfall records for the Rogue Valley, which he faithfully continued through June, 1863. According to his records, the average annual rain fall for the nine full years, was 18.43 inches. The highest year, 1861-62, was 34.48, and the lowest year, 1855-56, was 9.46 inches. His wife, Mary, would be recognized by Oregon Trail buffs, were she to reappear today, for her picture can be found on recent Oregon Trail brochures.

Cortez Myer's wife, Elizabeth, finished the quilt that she periodically pieced during the arduous trip to Oregon, but not until 1860. Because of its red and green poinsettia pattern, the quilt adorns our bed during the Christmas season. Their daughter, Frances, who was just a baby on the trip to Oregon, is Laura's grandmother.

Franklin Myer, a surveyor, officially platted much of land that comprised the town of Ashland. These surveys can still be found in abstracts of title that describe the boundaries and ownership of early day Ashland.

Nathaniel and Mary Myer are buried in a private cemetery in Valley View; probably on property that belonged to them.

Cortez and Elizabeth, along with their daughter, Frances and her husband, G.F. Billings, are buried in a family plot at the Hargadine cemetery, in Ashland. Mary Ann and John Walker's head-stones can be found nearby her brother's plot.

Franklin and Dorothy(Dolly) Myer, as well as his sister, Sarah Rockfellow, her husband, and children are buried in the Ashland cemetery.

Nathaniel's last diary entry, dated October 4, 1853 stated, "This day, Mother & my two youngest daughters and myself moved our beds into the cabin

Elizabeth Myer's quilt

Figure 53

build by my two sons for us; with the intention to sleep under a roof, which none of us did since the 23rd day of March last. The cabin is build of round logs, 14 by 16 feet. Stone chimey. Floor laid with good slabs from the mill. No door or class window; cloth is to be the substitute."

To our knowledge, Griffith Johns was never found, or brought to trial for the murder of Fruit Walker. Wondering about that, we may make him the subject of a future story of what might have happened!

KEN AND LAURA JONES

JANUARY 6, 1996

ABOUT THE AUTHORS

Born in Medford, Oregon, the year 1925, Ken Jones is a life long resident of Southern Oregon. Upon graduation from Medford High School in 1943, Ken joined the U.S. Army Air Corps, and received his wings, as a navigator, in 1944.

He married the former Laura Billings, also a native, just two days before V–J day in 1945. Upon graduation from the University of Oregon in 1948, Ken returned to Southern Oregon, joining his father in the Insurance business.

Now semi–retired, Ken stays busy as a tax consultant, and real estate investor, devoting the balance of his time to travel and writing.

Laura Billings Jones, born in Ashland, Oregon in 1926, is a descendent of the Myer family, who came to Ashland in covered wagons in 1853. Her grandmother, Frances Myer Billings, was age six months when the Myers began their Oregon Trail Journey. Laura's grandfather, G.F. Billings was a founder of the Chautauqua association in Ashland, serving as president for twenty two years. The "shell" housing the chautauqua is now a part of the world renowned Oregon Shakespeare Festival complex.

Laura, with Ken, has traveled throughout the U.S., Canada, Mexico, the Caribbean, and Europe. Her diaries and tape recordings provide the nucleus for their travel stories.

ADDITIONAL COPIES
AVAILABLE FROM:

Laura and Ken Jones
235 Terrace Street
Ashland, OR   97520-2834